CONTENTS

Prologue
Crisis in Genesis

It is said that the Chinese character for the word *crisis* is a combination of two characters, one meaning opportunity and the other meaning danger. I don't read Chinese myself; but if this is true, it aptly illustrates the nature of crisis. Often we see its negative aspect, danger. *Crisis* suggests times of pressure, testing, uncertainty, threat, and failure. Yet it is often in the midst of crisis that life is seen most clearly, that opportunities are grasped, and that greatness is achieved.

Genesis is filled with moments of crisis in individual lives. Adam and Eve are confronted with a crisis in relation to the tree of the knowledge of good and evil; Cain and Abel face a crisis in regard to their offerings to God; Noah faces a crisis in regard to the building of the ark; the people of Babel face a crisis in regard to their ambition in building a great tower; Abraham faces crises related to his journey of faith and the offering of his son; Sarah faces a crisis in regard to her advanced age and childlessness; Lot faces a crisis in relation to his residence in sinful Sodom; Isaac faces a crisis in regard to the blessing of his sons; Jacob faces a crisis in relation to his personal ambition and his ways of achieving success; Joseph faces a crisis in regard to his brothers' hatred for him and his response to it. Along with this company of the greats, there are the personal crises of people who play minor roles in the narrative. All of them are very like us and people we know.

While Genesis records actual events in the lives of real people, their lives are recorded to teach us lessons about God and His ways. In a very real sense, Old Testament history is designed as a picture book to illustrate universal spiritual truths. Paul wrote to the Corinthians, "All these things that happened to them were symbolic, and were recorded for our benefit as a warning. For upon us the fulfilment of the ages has come" (1 Corinthians 10:11, NEB). He likewise emphasized the instructional nature of the Old Testament by writing to the Romans, "For all the ancient Scriptures were written for our own instruction, in order that through the encouragement they give us we may maintain our hope with fortitude" (Romans 15:4, NEB). Those things that happened in the lives of Old Testament men and women picture for us what takes place spiritually in our own decisions, crises, commitments, temptations, and triumphs. Abraham illustrates justification by faith; Isaac illustrates the nature of trusting sonship; Jacob demonstrates deliverance from self-worship; Joseph portrays hope through death and resurrection.

In Genesis we read of good and bad choices that have had lasting consequences in human history. We are reminded that no man lives and dies in a vacuum, but that we are interlocked with those who have gone before us and those who will follow us. This book is titled *Crisis in Genesis*. Like Genesis itself, that title is intended to cut two ways. First, it indicates the book is a study of the Bible book of Genesis, viewing it in particular as a series of crises that reveal, as the Chinese character implies, both opportunity for faithfulness and danger of sin. Second, the title points to the fact that the crises encountered by the men and women in the Bible book of Genesis are prototypical. The things recorded in Genesis are not merely past history. They are present realities in us. We study Genesis not only to know the ancients, but also to know ourselves.

Genesis is a dramatic book. It is a book of action, moving quickly from event to event. It does not pause often to reflect on the meaning of the actions it records. This is one reason for its fascination. The human drama of individuals under stress is perpetually captivating, as the popularity of violent drama and TV soap operas well illustrates. While Genesis does not pause often to comment on significance, the remainder of the Bible is, in a real sense, a commentary on that significance. As we study Genesis, we will try not to impede the flow of action; but we will pause now and then to reflect on the meanings for our time.

Genesis is a book of people. In its pages the record of man's habitation of the earth is unfolded from its earliest beginnings. It should be remembered, however, that Genesis is not a scientific or philosophical look at the great questions that occupy men's minds and hearts. Rather it is a personal, biographically-centered look at these questions. The focus is upon the human encounter, the personal decision, and the pivotal action. Genesis is not an abstract treatise on being. It is rather the story of beings who, whether saints or sinners, have embodied lasting lessons for all subsequent human strugglers. From the triumphs and defeats of our physical and spiritual ancestors, let us learn lessons of eternal significance.

1

Crisis
In Identity
Genesis 1, 2

Who are we? Why are we here? How are we like the other things in this world, and how are we different? What is the purpose of human life, and, in particular, our own personal lives? If there are purpose and meaning in human life, how can we know what they are?

These are timeless questions pondered by thinking humans long before the invention of our modern term *identity crisis*. The answers we accept have far-reaching effects on the way we conduct our lives. Throughout history man's basic spiritual and social problems have been related to the fact that many people do not know where they came from, who they are, what they want, why they exist, to whom they are responsible, and where they are going. To be without concrete and satisfying answers to these questions is to be awash in a sea of uncertainty, aimlessness, and despair.

The book of Genesis takes us back to our beginnings. It not only tells us how we came to be, but also what we are intended to be. In our twentieth-century search for meaningful existence, there is no better place to begin than at the beginning.

The focus of the opening verse and the opening chapters of Genesis is on God. He alone is eternally pre-existent, without beginning and without end. He is unlike all other things that we come to know. It is He who brings matter into existence, who brings order out of chaos, and who forms the celestial bodies and the geographical features of the earth. It is God who fashions the animals with all their wonderful variety. It is God who designs the plants, fitting them so perfectly to earth's atmospheric system and to man's need for food. It is God who forms the sea creatures, the air creatures, and the land creatures to mate and multiply and to be subservient to the needs of His human creation.

The emphasis at the beginning of the "book of beginnings" is on God. Our attention is quickly drawn, however, to His creative activity. He is not merely impersonal energy or force; He is master designer, prime mover, infinite provider, speaker of light and life, organizer, divider, namer, observer, initiator, maker, blesser, commander, and ordainer. God, in the opening chapter of Genesis, is defined not by abstractions but by concrete action. It is action, moreover, that He alone is capable of. The world is designed and crafted by a God who can by the very power of His word shape firmaments, move waters, cause vegetation to spring forth, and populate the seas and dry land with a huge variety of living creatures. Our world and the universe are the conscious creation of this personal, rational God of action.

There are, of course, many things that our questing minds would like to know about God's methodology in creation. Creatures of time that we are, we are particularly curious about the temporal nature of God's creative processes. The Hebrew historian, however, is more concerned with the Who than with the how of creation. He desires that we know in no uncertain terms that God, not time and chance, is responsible for all that makes our earth hospitable for human habitation.

Many insights into reality can be found in the opening chapters of Genesis, but six things are especially evident. We state them briefly here, and then will discuss them a little in the six sections that follow in this chapter:

1. Men and women bear the image of God (1:26a, 27).
2. Men and women have natures that are both material and spiritual (1:27; 2:7).
3. Men and women are born to rule (1:26b).
4. Men and women are created for companionship (1:27; 2:18-25; 3:8).
5. Men and women are classifiers and organizers (2:19, 20a).
6. Mankind is one (2:7).

10

Men and Women Bear the Image of God
1:26a, 27

God said, "Let Us make man in Our image, according to Our likeness" (NASB). To us egocentric humans, this passage is infinitely interesting. This truth goes far to explain the uniqueness of human nature and to satisfy our quest for significant identity. Man, bearing the stamp of God's image, exists on a level above all other earthly creatures. He has been created with a nature capable of feeling, reasoning, judging, willing, wanting, needing, giving, and loving.

Man is like the animals in some ways. In fact, in some ways he is like the plants, and even like the earth from which he was made. But he is also different from any of these.

Man's moral nature, his reasoning ability, and his emotional makeup set him apart from the rest of creation. This "inner man," with all its potential for greatness, reflects in human form the very nature of the Creator of the universe. Without this essential similarity and alikeness, man and God could not share meaningful communication, interaction, and love. We can communicate, to a limited extent, with animals; but few of us would enjoy an evening discussing Shakespeare with a pet schnauzer. In order for there to be meaningful communication, a similarity of natures is essential.

Men and Women Have Natures
That Are Both Material and Spiritual
1:27; 2:7

Man is made of material substance. His body is composed of the elements of the earth. He is tangible and recognizable. He also consists of immaterial substance, life. God is the source of both matter and life. It was God's breath that activated or inspired clay into living creature.

Scholars are careful to note that the statement, "Man became a living soul," does not call attention to the soul dimension that distinguishes man from animal. It is the same Hebrew expression that is translated "life" and "living creature" in 1:20, 21, 24, 30, where it applies to animals. God's breath of life made man a *living being*. Like the animals of God's creation, man is an animated creature. It is the "image of God" in man that gives him soul-dimension and sets him apart from all other inhabitants of this planet (1:27). The thought of 2:7 is that man owes his existence to God. As Paul put it to the Athenians on Mars Hill, "In Him we live and move and exist" (Acts 17:28, NASB).

11

Men and Women Are Born to Rule
1:26b

God gave man dominion over all the other creatures. Slower than many, weaker than some, more fragile than most, man nevertheless found himself ruler over the beasts. God gave man dominion over the plants of the earth as well. Even in the beginning, the plants needed to be looked after (2:15). Man had something to occupy his mind and challenge his efforts.

But the world was more than man's "sandbox." It was an integrated, interlocking system in which man found himself in a special relationship with all living and nonliving things on the face of the earth.

The history of man has been the history of his exercise of dominion. The fuse of the population explosion was lit by the command, "Be fruitful, and multiply, and replenish the earth." The rush toward the technological age began with the command, "Subdue it: and have dominion."

Men and Woman Are Created for Companionship
1:27; 2:18-25; 3:8

We are not explicitly told *why* God created man. We can only guess that something in the divine nature sought the companionship of a free, thinking creation.

There are companionship, love, and interaction among the Father, Son, and Holy Spirit. There are communication and interaction between God and the angels. But from *our* point of view, His companionship with mankind is the most important companionship of all.

Being made in the image of God, man was a being suited for companionship. Adam needed a companion suitable for him, like but unlike him, complementing and fulfilling him. Unlike Adam, who was formed from the dust of the earth, Eve was formed from Adam. This underlines the essential unity and oneness of God's human creation. Man and woman were not independent, competing creatures. What had been one became two. In the marriage relationship that God designed for them, those two would become one again (2:24).

Men and Woman Are Classifiers and Organizers
2:19, 20a

It is worth noting that one of man's first tasks was the naming of things. God and man were communicating in language, so far as we know. God gave names to day and night, heaven and earth and seas (1:5-10). But God did not take man by the hand, like a guide in a zoological garden, and say, "This is what I call a giraffe; this is what I call an alligator; this is what I call an aardvark." Man himself was given responsibility for building language. From the beginning man has been an identifier, an encoder, a definer, and a classifier.

The task begun by Adam has continued as one of man's major preoccupations. We are constantly on the lookout for new things, or old things that are new to us because we have not observed them before: new animal species, new planets, new plants, new concepts, new scientific observations, and new ways of defining our experience. Libraries are filled with books designed to name and define the phenomena of human experience. Colleges thrive on their special nomenclature and learned jargon. God and Adam began a process that continues to occupy and fascinate mankind.

Mankind Is One
2:7

A quick look at *National Geographic* alerts us to the fact that there are profound differences in the people of this world. We see the fantastically varied customs, costumes, beliefs, and habits of the fascinating human dwellers of this earth. Yet beneath this great diversity is a common source and identity. We are all God's creatures, uniquely created in His image, sharing common ancestry in Adam and Eve, designed for companionship with one another and with God. Wide as the gulf is between the Aborigine in Australia and the broker in Boston, a basic unity of being is present that sets human creatures apart from all else. Genesis reminds us of the essential unity of all mankind.

Crisis and Struggle

All these human characteristics provide man with arenas for struggle and crisis.

Man is in the image of God, but sin has marred that image. Man was created for companionship, but men and women are alienated from God and from one another. Mankind struggles with the weight of sin and the consciousness that all have fallen from the purity of nature with which mankind began. We struggle with the essence of our being, often painfully conscious of the conflict between our spiritual and physical natures.

Man finds crisis, turmoil, and heartache in his interpersonal relationships. He struggles with the implications of companionship. His loves bring turmoil and his interactions with others bring bewilderment and distress.

Man, the organizer and identifier, struggles to know ever more, often to the point of deifying his methods of learning. He labors to discover and use to his advantage new things, then struggles to remain free from the tyranny of his creations. He struggles with his stewardship of the earth and its resources.

God, the Mooring of Our Identity

It is clear from Genesis that it is impossible to understand who we are and for what we exist without acknowledging the sovereignity and primacy of God. We exist by His will and we are sustained by His provision. It is He that has made us and not we ourselves. Two great truths shine forth: *God creates* and *God cares*. If we find ourselves living without purpose, discouraged with life, and defeated by circumstances, we must turn our minds and hearts once again to communion with God and consideration of the companionship with Him and with one another for which He created us.

For Reflection

1. Read Genesis 1 and make a list of the different things God does. What do these activities reveal about His nature?

2. Read Genesis 1 again and make a list of phrases that are often repeated. Why do you think this is done?

3. How do you understand the statement that man is created in God's image? What implications does this have for man?

4. What problems in your life would be diminished or solved if you would acknowledge more completely the primacy and sovereignty of God?

5. What beliefs in our society are contrary to the truths presented in this Scripture? What implications do these beliefs have for morality, conduct, and purpose for life?

6. How does man exercise dominion over the earth? What abuses of this mandate do you observe as you look at man's use of his environment?

7. What do we learn about the relationship of husband and wife from this Scripture?

8. What commands of God are heard in Genesis 1 and 2? What

prohibition? Does the prohibition seem incompatible with the goodness of the things of the garden? Why or why not?

9. Is scientific knowledge incompatible with faith and close relationship with God?

10. What things in Genesis 1 and 2 most impress you? What meaning do these things have for our present day?

Perspectives on the Identity Crisis

- There is divine design both in the universe and in the individual.
- We cannot understand our purpose on earth without understanding our relationship with God.
- Men and women were created as complements of one another, not as rivals.
- God brings order to chaos, light to darkness, fruitfulness to life, and goodness to all things He touches.
- Ought we not to give careful attention to the words of Him who spoke the universe into existence?
- I am important because of God's love for me, not because of my own merit, beauty, or intelligence.
- "So God created man in his own image, in the image of God created he him; male and female created he them" (Genesis 1:27).

2

Crisis
in freedom[1]
Genesis 3

Harmony

Adam and Eve were created in the image of God. They were placed in a good creation. They spent their days tending and caring for the luxuriant garden. The plants responded to their care and filled their lives with beauty and abundant food. Man's life was characterized by harmony. Chapter 2 of Genesis ends with two words that describe man's harmonious condition—"not ashamed." Created to complement one another, the first man and woman were in harmony with one another. Most importantly, however, they were in harmony with God. It seems to have been His custom to walk and talk with them in the cool of the evening (3:8).

A day of crisis, however, was to come to the garden. Peace and harmony were never to exist in quite the same way again.

Choice

God loved His human creation, and human creation existed to love God. When asked which was the great commandment of the law, Jesus later was to say, "Thou shalt love the Lord thy God with

---

1. Portions of this chapter are taken from *Triumph Over Temptation,* Standard Publishing Co., 1984. That book, by the present author, explores in detail Biblical teaching on the subject of temptation.

all thy heart, and with all thy soul, and with all thy mind" (Matthew 22:37).

Yet man was no automaton, built in such a way that he could do nothing but what God desired of him. Man was created with freedom of choice. Without choice, his love for God and his obedience to God would have been meaningless.

The relationship between God and man was never one of equal with equal. God was Creator; man was creature. Love of Creator by creature involved recognition of the creature's dependence, submission, and obedience.

It was not by chance that there was a prohibition in the garden (2:16, 17). Man's freedom required something like that tree—a place of choice. The "tree of the knowledge of good and evil" was the place at which man was confronted with the responsibilities of freedom. There he could choose to believe God and love Him as His creature should, or he could choose to become autonomous and independent, supplanting the Creator. Without such a possibility of disobedience, man's obedience and love would have been hollow.

With the creation of the tree of the knowledge of good and evil, God voluntarily placed choice in man's world. It was a risky thing, but it was necessary to reveal the full significance of man as he was intended to be—free and voluntarily loving. Without choice, all love as we know it is empty, whether it be between a man and a woman or between friends. Choice, likewise, is a vital ingredient in man's relationship with God.

We noted earlier the harmony of the garden: man in harmony with himself; man in harmony with his environment; man harmonizing with his human counterpart; man harmonizing with his Creator. That special tree, that tree of the knowledge of good and evil, was harmoniously fitted to the inner nature of man as a free and independent being. Further, this "tree of choice," holding within it the promise of death, was balanced by the tree of life (2:9).

Command
God left no uncertainty about the "choice tree." He explained clearly what the result of disobedience would be (2:17). God gave mankind one prohibition, one "thou shalt not." The outcome of disobedience would be death.

We are left to ponder the implications of this negative command for Adam and Eve. What could they understand of death at this point? They had not yet observed human death firsthand. We are not told that they had seen it in the animal world yet either. Did God explain to them the meaning of death? And what about their moral nature before the fall? We read that one of the results of the fall was that they knew good and evil in a different way (3:22). What was their level of understanding before the fall?

We will talk more about this question later. Suffice it to say here that before the fall man had a consciousness of right and wrong at least to the extent that he knew that to go against God's command would be wrong. He knew right and wrong, not from having experienced wrong, but from God's identification of it.

Doubt

Temptation entered the Garden of Eden in the form of a Satan-controlled serpent. The serpent, one of God's good creatures, became a means of accomplishing Satan's evil purposes. Temptation came cunningly. Clothed as one of the lesser creatures, Satan subverted the crowning creature. Satan, we learn in Scripture, is the enemy of both God and man (Matthew 13:39), the adversary (1 Peter 5:8), the tempter (Matthew 4:3; 1 Thessalonians 3:5), the father of lies (John 8:44), the deceiver (Revelation 12:9), an accuser (Revelation 12:10), a murderer (John 8:44), and the wicked one (Matthew 13:19; 1 John 2:13, 14; 3:12; 5:18). The Bible further declares that Satan disguises himself as an angel of light (2 Corinthians 11:14). To Eve he disguised himself as an angel of enlightenment.

Satan's first question to Eve, on the surface, seemed innocent enough. "Is it true," he said, "that God has prohibited you from eating of any tree of the garden?" He knew it was; he wasn't asking for information. The question, very likely, was filled with pretended incredulity. "Surely God has not given *you* a prohibition. Don't tell me that your loving Creator is holding something back from *you*, of all creatures!"

Satan wanted the woman to look at the tree from the wrong perspective. The tree stood, in God's good provision, as a blessing through which a free moral agent could demonstrate a faith-relationship with God. Satan wanted Eve to view this prohibition as an unnecessary, unfair impingement on her personal freedom.

Eve was drawn into this apparently sympathetic conversation with Satan. He seemed so genuinely interested in her welfare. Her reply to him began well enough. It called attention to the fact that God had provided all that she needed by means of the other trees of the garden (3:2). However, there may have been some hint of amazement at the ways of God in the latter part of her reply (3:3). Not only did she call attention to the commandment of God that no one eat of the "revolt tree"; she also added that God had prohibited even the touching of it, on fear of death. Some commentators suggest that Eve was already beginning to take things into her own hands by presuming to add to God's commandment. They see her as questioning the stringency of God's attitude in the matter: "Would you believe it? We can't even *touch* it!" Whether or not this is reading too much into her words, it is clear that at some point Eve began to flirt with doubt about the love and provision of God. Doubt marked the beginning of her fall. Doubt, in its turn, led to denial. Denial led to death.

Something in Eve's reply told Satan that she was ready for the big lie. She had begun to see the obedience tree as somehow in contradiction with God's love. Satan succeeded in getting her to wonder at the prohibition rather than the provision of the garden. Satan still uses that tactic. He wants us to look disappointedly at what God asks us to avoid rather than to look thankfully at what He provides, hoping to make us believe that what is withheld is really better for us than what is given.

Denial

God had said that the tree of choice held within it the possibility of death. Satan, however, called God a liar. "You surely shall not die!" Satan said. Since the lie was cast in the realm of the future, Eve had to decide between God and Satan on the basis of faith.

This was a critical moment for Eve. Did she turn away in scorn from this contradiction of her Creator? Did she recoil in horror from this rebellious thought? She, unfortunately, did not.

Satan still persists in pulling this deception. How frequently, in our day, we hear that God's revelation is not true to reality as we moderns know it. Satan asserts that God is not the source of truth and the understanding of life. But anything that discredits God is false. Will we never learn that?

Lies are always more convincing when supported by half-truths. "Ye shall be as gods, knowing good and evil," Satan declared (3:5). Eve interpreted that promise, as Satan intended that she would, to be a desirable thing. She was to learn, to her sorrow, that it is actually a terrible thing.

In Genesis 3:22 we hear God saying, after the fall, "Behold, the man is become as one of us, to know good and evil." "What is wrong with that?" we ask. "Isn't it desirable to know the difference between good and evil? Doesn't God want us to have discerning ability so that we will identify and shun evil? Didn't Eve purchase for mankind a valuable gift through her disobedience?" Most decidedly not!

We have suggested that before the fall Adam and Eve had enough moral sense for God to appeal to it with His negative commandment concerning the tree. But at that point they did not have *experiential knowledge* of evil. They did not know evil from having done it. That was the new knowledge that brought alienation and death.

The Scriptures say that Adam and Eve became like God, knowing good and evil. Just how does God know evil? Certainly He does not know it, as Adam and Eve eventually did, from having done it. Ray Stedman, commenting on this question, wrote:

> God knows evil, not by experience, because he cannot experience evil, but by relating it to himself. That which is consistent with his character and his nature is good; that which is inconsistent with it is evil. That which is out of line, out of character with himself, is evil, destructive, and dangerous; but all that is in line with his own nature is good. That is how God "knows" good and evil. He relates it to himself.
>
> But God is the only one who can properly do that. God is the only Being in all the universe who has the right to relate all things to himself. When a creature tries it he gets into trouble. The creatures of God's universe are made to discover the difference between good and evil by relating all to the Being of God, not to themselves. When man ate of the fruit he began to do what God does—to relate everything to himself.... When man began to think of himself as the center of the universe, he became like God. But it was all a lie. Man is not the center of the universe, and he cannot be.[2]

Satan still uses that lie today. He whispers in our ears that what we think is right is all that matters: there are no absolute rights or wrongs, he says; what we want to do is right and what we don't want to do is wrong.

---

2. Ray C. Stedman, *Understanding Man*, copyright © 1974, pp. 35, 36; used by permission of Word Books, Publisher, Waco, Texas 76796.

The Eden testing tree was a place for the opportunity of experientially knowing good and experientially knowing evil. Until the fall, both Adam and Eve experientially knew good. As they trusted in God and listened to His instructions, *all* was good. It was the *experience of evil* that they were to learn by disobedience. Satan made that seem good, but it was not. As Francis Schaeffer wrote:

> It is true that Eve is indeed going to learn something. If she chooses to disobey and to rebel, she will have what she couldn't have had otherwise—an experiential knowledge of evil and its results. So in a way Satan is telling her the truth. But what a useless, horrible knowledge! It is the knowledge of the child whose mother says, "Don't go near that fire, because if you do you will get hurt. You will catch fire and be burned." But the little child goes on in disobedience, falls into the fire and spends the next three days dying in agony. The child has learned something that it wouldn't have known experientially if it had listened to the knowledge given by its mother. But what a knowledge![3]

God certainly wants us to be like Him. The way to that, however, is never disobedience to His commands. Satan promises freedom through disobedience to God; it comes, however, only through obedience to Him.

Crisis

Eve was moving toward crisis just as surely as she walked through the luxurious vegetation of the garden. Eve's mind was no longer on all that God provided for her. It was on the forbidden tree only.

There she stood before it, looking at it, thinking about it, weighing what Satan had said. Doubt had been planted in her mind—doubt that continued to be tended and nurtured. She was savoring the forbidden idea; soon she would be savoring the forbidden fruit. Far from being repugnant, the tree was attractive to Eve in every way (3:6). The tree appealed to her appetite, a good, God-given thing. She had been designed with the ability to taste and enjoy, to savor and appreciate, to smell and relish. The fruit not only seemed quite

---

3. From Francis Schaeffer, *Genesis in Space and Time*, 1972. Used by permission of L'Abri Fellowship, Switzerland. Permission granted by InterVarsity Press, U.S.A., p. 81.

edible and delectable to the taste buds, it looked beautiful to the eye as well. Her God-given aesthetic sense, designed by God to make her appreciative of His work of creative genius, became the instrument of her rationalization of evil. Her aspiration for wisdom, a God-given mental faculty, was used by Satan to defeat true wisdom. (See Proverbs 9:10.)

In all of this Satan capitalized on human drives and appetites to corroborate his deadly deceptions. All Eve's senses were now "go." Her senses of smell and taste said, "Yes, satisfy your hungers." Her sense of sight said, "By all means indulge yourself." Her sense of hearing, jammed by Satan's lies and half-truths, said, "Grab for the forbidden prize." All that remained was the sense of touch. . . .

She touched the forbidden tree. Nothing seemed to happen. (If touching had not been prohibited, but had been her own addition to the command, perhaps she was encouraged by this first step.) Then, "She took of the fruit thereof, and did eat" (Genesis 3:6).

Like many a transgressor since, Eve immediately looked for someone to share in her sin. She became a "pusher." She wanted Adam to join her, and he did. (It is true today that the person who gives himself to disobedience to God becomes an advocate for his sinful life-style. There is nothing that bothers the sinner more than for others to reject his rationalization of evil conduct. He will seek to infect others with the fatal virus of sin. Our newsstands are filled with the writings of those who would push their degradation on others, presenting it as mind-, spirit-, and sense-expanding freedom rather than the deadly enslavement it is.) Satan became Eve's silent partner, delighted that now she was a willing accomplice in his death-dealing business. Instead of using her relationship with Adam to help him in his relationship with God, Eve became Satan's instrument in Adam's downfall. Instead of Adam's using his relationship with her to help her return to a right relationship with God, he joined her in sin.

While much is said in this passage about how Eve was deceived, very little is said about the process by which Adam joined Eve outside the limitations of God. Men, always looking for a high motive to justify a low act, would like to believe that he crossed over the line to share the fate of the woman he loved. Yet it seems somehow more casual than that. The Bible says she "gave also unto her husband with her; and he did eat" (3:6). It sounds as if he thoughtlessly treated the violation of God's command as a matter of little consequence.

Shame

The eyes of Adam and Eve were opened, not to the anticipated benefits of disobedience, but to guilt and shame. A self-consciousness replaced God-consciousness. Suddenly they found themselves naked, and they did not like it. Their shame of body was an outward expression of a shame of soul. Like many a sinner since, they initiated a futile cover-up. They sewed fig leaves together to hide themselves from one another (3:7). A separation was taking place between Adam and Eve. Not only did this pair seek to hide themselves from one another, they sought to hide themselves from God (3:8).

They didn't like the look of themselves; they didn't like the look of each other; and they didn't like the look of God. Sin authors self-deception, other-deception, and God-deception. Though they tried to cover themselves, they were unsuccessful in hiding from God. As the writer to the Hebrews put it, "There is nothing in creation that can hide from him; everything lies naked and exposed to the eyes of the One with whom we have to reckon" (Hebrews 4:13, NEB).

No longer was the evening presence of God the most desired moment of the day for Adam and Eve. In sin, they felt exposed before their all-knowing Creator. For the first time in history, God's presence was something to fear (3:8-10). By yielding to Satan's lies, they had altered their thinking about God. Now He was no longer a loving companion, a partner in creative endeavor, and a provider of good. Rather He was the unwelcome voice of justice and truth, truth that they no longer wanted to hear.

When God said, "Where are you?" Adam did not reply with a geographical location. He replied in terms of his inner state. He was afraid; he was ashamed. He was in a state of mind and spirit where he wanted most of all to escape the view of God.

God confronted Adam with his sin, asking from whom he was getting his information: "Who told thee that thou wast naked? Hast thou eaten of the tree, whereof I commanded thee that thou shouldest not eat?" (3:11).

Like many a sinner since, Adam responded by blaming someone else (3:12). Further, he blamed God who had given Eve to him in the first place. Eve followed the same game plan. She blamed the serpent and, by implication, God who had created the serpent and put it in the garden (3:13). (Man's reluctance to take responsibility for sin thrives today. We blame parents, society, external forces of all kinds, and ultimately God for what we deem as faulty workmanship in the nature of God's creation—anything to avoid personal responsibility.)

23

There is something in all this that touches the very core of our natures. We ache in our bones for something that no longer exists, a relationship of perfect peace with God and man. We are no longer creatures completely at home with ourselves, with our environment, and with God.

Death

The sin of this first pair brought about a separation from God, which might be described as living death. They continued to breathe; their hearts continued to beat; but they already had begun to collect the wages of sin. As the countdown of their allotted time began, physical death became a fact of life. And eternal death also lay as a possibility on the horizon of mankind (2 Thessalonians 1:9).

Disharmony and Hope

Nature itself was altered. The serpent was no longer good in the eyes of man. It was destined to be a cursed reminder of the depths to which man had fallen (3:14, 15).

The harmony of the man-woman relationship was altered. Pain and sorrow would accompany childbirth; woman would be subservient to man (3:16). Nature would no longer be beneficent. Man would live in a world of difficulty. Thorns and thistles in the natural world, and sweat and unmitigated toil in the human world, were to be the new order of things (3:17-19).

In the midst of the tragic aftermath of the fall, however, there is the faint glow of hope. It is hidden away in the curse of the serpent in Genesis 3:15. One of Eve's descendants would bruise the head of the serpent, while the serpent would bruise His heel. This is the first prophecy of God's redemptive work to be accomplished in His Son, Jesus. God incarnate, Jesus the Christ, born of woman, would in the fullness of time conquer Satan and death by His crucifixion and resurrection.

We generally see the things of Genesis 3:14-19 as curses. That is certainly part of their nature, but it is not all. They seem designed by God as part of His gracious plan to bring man back to loving relationship with Him.

Pain ("Why does God permit suffering in the world?"), submission ("Why can't a person do what he pleases?"), toil ("Why is nature so hostile to man?"), and death ("Why did my loved one have to die?") are primary testing points in the lives of each of us. Most people who choose not to believe in God choose from among these reasons

24

for their disbelief. Yet each of these areas affords tremendous opportunity for demonstrating trust in God. We have opportunity to use these conditions, through Christ, as a means for developing the trusting character God wants of us and for doing what Adam and Eve failed to do, overcoming the deceits of Satan and the rebelliousness of our natures.

We should note that immediately after God's curse of death (3:19) and before man's separation from the tree of life (3:22-24), God made for Adam and Eve clothes of animal skins. Perhaps this was their first experiential contact with death—the death of an animal foreshadowing their own now certain deaths. It may be in this also that we see God teaching Adam and Eve the nature of blood sacrifice and the covering it represents. Other than this note, we are not told in the Bible when the idea of blood sacrifice began. We do learn, however, in Genesis 4, that Adam and Eve's children knew about it. All of this, of course, provides understanding of the perfect sacrifice of Jesus that covers and takes away our sin (1 Peter 1:18, 19; 1 John 1:7; Revelation 1:5; 7:14).

This chapter has much to teach us about freedom and responsibility, about our rebelliousness, and about our guilt and self-consciousness. We long for the things of the world: the lust of the flesh, the lust of the eyes, and the pride of life (1 John 2:16). We, like Adam and Eve, frequently seek independence from God, only to find ourselves enslaved by sin and lamenting its fallout in our lives. Like Eve, we fall in love with forbidden things and begin to want Satan's lies to be true. When we sin, we excuse ourselves and point the finger at others. Yet even in our disobedience, God comes to us in love. In Adam came death, but in Christ comes life (1 Corinthians 15:22).

For Reflection

1. Why do you think the tree of the knowledge of good and evil was in the Garden of Eden?

2. In what sense was Satan's assertion in Genesis 3:5 true? (Compare 3:22.) In what sense was it false?

3. Why do you think Eve began to listen to Satan rather than to God? Why do we do this? What reasons did Eve have *for* listening to God? What reasons do we have?

4. Why do you think Eve was so quick to involve her husband in disobedience? What do you think were *his* motives?

5. What were the immediate results of their sin? What did they try to do?

6. How did Adam and Eve seek to evade responsibility? Whom did they see as primarily at fault? In what ways do we today continue in this evasion?

7. Genesis 2:17 says, "For in the day that thou eatest thereof thou shalt surely die." How can this be reconciled with the fact that Adam and Eve did not immediately fall down dead when they disobeyed?

8. What were the curses connected with the fall? How were they designed for man's good?

9. Explain the Messianic hope of Genesis 3:15.

10. What remedy is there for the sin that came into the world with the fall?

Perspectives on the Freedom Crisis

• Freedom and responsibility—the two are linked together like the two faces of a coin.

• Many human problems, past and present, are related to man's inability to handle freedom.

• It was impossible for man to be truly loving toward God without being truly free. It was impossible for man to be truly free without there being the possibility of disobedience.

• Disobedience fractured the harmony of the good world that God created.

• In spite of what Satan says, God always speaks the truth.

• Satan beguiles us with questions, which grow into doubts, which grow into enticing desires, which grow into sinful deeds. He works with half-truths and whole lies. He appeals to our fleshly appetites, our materialistic desires, and our pride. He offers liberated life; he delivers death.

• "The man that wandereth out of the way of understanding shall remain in the congregation of the dead" (Proverbs 21:16).

• "If the Son therefore shall make you free, ye shall be free indeed" (John 8:36).

3

Crisis
in brotherhood
Genesis 3:22 – 5:32

Mankind was now fatally flawed. Adam and Eve had not been able to handle freedom. They had disobeyed God and striven for God-likeness on their own terms, not God's. Adam and Eve had been separated from each other, from nature, and from God. They found themselves exposed, guilty before God, and driven from paradise. They were also soon to learn, in the lives of their sons, the tragic truth that sin begets sin.

Sacrifice
In Genesis 3:21 we learn that God made Adam and Eve clothes of animal skins. Perhaps this was the first sight of death ever to be witnessed in the garden. Some scholars suggest that in this way God showed the first couple how they could use their sovereignty over animals for their own benefit.

In sacrificing animal life for the preservation of human life, God laid the foundation for all succeeding sacrifices by which men and women sought to restore broken relationships with God. Man's improvised leaf covering was not enough. Man's true covering required sacrifice and death. God provided it here in the animal skins; He would ultimately provide it in the death of His own Son. The sacrifice of animals pictures the idea, but only the sacrifice of Jesus could really take away sin (Hebrews 10:3-10).

Cain and Abel

It was in connection with sacrifice that the next crisis of obedience came. Eve bore a son. Her exclamation, "I have gotten a man from the Lord," seems filled with joy and awe. Her son had not been created and given to her fully grown. He had been born in the pain of natural childbirth, but Eve clearly recognized that the source of all life was God. It was the Lord who had given her a son. His parents called their first son Cain, "begotten," perhaps in recognition of the first human birth (4:1).

Soon a second son was born. He was called Abel. Some see his name as a variation of the word for shepherd. Others trace it to a word meaning breath or vapor, thus suggesting his brief existence and tragic end. Still others think that it referred to the ease of this second birth for Eve.

Children can be a joy to their parents, and we have no reason to believe that Cain and Abel were otherwise for Adam and Eve. Adam was both a herdsman and a tiller of the ground, but each of his sons gradually gravitated toward different activity, Abel to herding the flocks, Cain to farming. Specialization, it seems, is of ancient origin.

Offering

One day these two sons stood before God with offerings. The Scriptures don't record how they came to know that this would be pleasing to God, nor are we told of specific instructions concerning their offerings. We can assume that they learned about worship from their parents. The sons, Scripture tells us, came with the produce of their disparate vocations (4:3, 4a).

Cain brought the produce of the fields; Abel brought the best from his flocks. God honored Abel's sacrifice, but He was displeased with the offering of the elder brother, Cain (4:4b, 5a). We are not told precisely why God was displeased with Cain's offering. Was it because God had specifically commanded a blood sacrifice? (Hebrews 9:22). Had Cain knowingly tried to substitute his "own thing"? Or was it that Abel brought the fittest, fattest, and finest to the Lord, while Cain brought the ordinary and poor from his fields? Or did Cain bring only a handful, not a tithe?

Or then again, was the difference one of attitude? Was Abel's offering given in deep abiding faith in contrast to Cain's grudging and superficial attitude? (Hebrews 11:4). We cannot be sure. But the result, whatever the cause, was that God was displeased with Cain. Cain was at a point of crisis.

Sin at the Door

Cain had two alternatives. Confronted with his error, he could humbly return to God with a suitable offering. God held that way open to him: "If thou doest well, shalt thou not be accepted?" (4:7). God was willing for Cain to profit from this experience.

Cain, however, chose the other alternative. He was angry. He pouted. He was crestfallen. Instead of searching himself to see what was wrong, he struck out at his brother who, he felt, had made him look bad (4:5b). If God asked an animal sacrifice, Cain could please Him by trading some of his grain to his shepherd brother for a sacrificial lamb. But that must have seemed humiliating to him. A man's work tends to become an extension of himself. To trade the product of his own work for a lamb of his brother's flock may have seemed to Cain to mean that he was inferior. It also meant yielding his own self-will to the will of God.

God warned Cain that sin was lurking like a hungry animal at the door of his heart, but he could still conquer and overcome by following the course of obedience (4:6, 7). But Cain opened the door to sin, and it proceeded to devour him. Exposed in disobedience, guilty before God, mankind has two choices—repentance or the disclaiming of personal responsibility. Cain chose this latter course. His guilt produced pride and jealousy, which in turn gave way to anger, hatred, and murder.

Anger, as we know all too well, needs a focus. Cain could not be angry with God, for God had treated him with mercy. He refused to be angry with himself. So he focused his anger on his innocent brother, whom he resented for his faithfulness and his approval by God. John wrote, "For this is the message that ye heard from the beginning, that we should love one another. Not as Cain, who was of that wicked one, and slew his brother. And wherefore slew he him? Because his own works were evil, and his brother's righteous" (1 John 3:11, 12).

All of this would be hard for us to understand if there were not so much of Cain in each of us. Envy, jealousy, bitterness, and backbiting are far too common in our own hearts for us to be surprised to see them in the hearts of our ancestors.

Death

The curse of disobedience in the Garden of Eden was death. And the curse of disobedience outside the garden was also death. Death came to Abel at the hands of his brother. Cain himself joined the ranks of the living dead. As John later was to put it, "He that loveth not his brother abideth in death" (1 John 3:14).

Cain killed Abel in the fields, perhaps purposefully selecting a place where the deed could be well hidden (4:8). Like his parents before him, however, he was to learn that his deeds could not be hidden from God.

My Brother's Brother

The Lord asked a question of Cain. It reminds us of the question He asked Cain's parents in the garden. Then He asked, "Where are you?" Here He asked, "Where is your brother?" (4:9a).

Cain's reply has become proverbial (4:9b). It showed disdain for both God and his brother. Cain followed the road of error, unrepentance, sin, and defiance. He moved inexorably toward the point of punishment.

Cain was listening to God at this point, but he did not hear something that God heard distinctly. Abel's blood was crying, as it were, from the ground where it fell. Cain had arranged things so there had been no witnesses. But his brother's blood bore witness against him, crying out for judgment (4:10). Nothing, Cain was learning, escaped God. The writer of Hebrews contrasts the blood of Abel with the blood of Jesus. Abel's blood called for judgment, but Jesus' blood speaks of forgiveness, love, and mercy (Hebrews 12:24).

Judgment

God gave judgment. The very earth that Cain defiled with blood would no longer yield abundantly to his hand. Cain, the green-thumbed farmer who took pride in his ability to grow things, sowed blood in his fields. Those fields would never again yield abundantly to his blood-stained hands (4:11, 12). The good farmer's life is stationary. Perhaps that is one thing Cain liked about it. The bad farmer's life is transient. Unable to make the land yield, Cain would be forever moving on, forever looking for a new place to plant. Where formerly he had enjoyed the settled life of a farmer, walking happily in his prosperous fields, now he would be an outcast and a vagabond, a fugitive and wanderer. Both the earth and its inhabitants would be hostile to him. Cain's experience would give a name to the east country where he would be a nomad. It is called the land of Nod, the land of wandering (4:16).

FEAR

Still Cain did not repent and ask forgiveness. Without remorse for his fratricide, without admitting the great wrong he had done not only to his blood brother but to one made in God's image, he thought only of himself, protesting that God's punishment was too severe (4:13, 14).

Cain, who had so brutally taken the life of his brother, was very concerned for *his own life*. The murderer now saw a world full of avengers. Not only would he spend his life hounded by loneliness, he also would be hounded by fear. Always with an eye over his shoulder, Cain walked the earth a marked man, the captive of his own disregard for life and brotherhood. His own relatives would be set against him, whether from distrust, fear, or a desire for vengeance.

The Mark

God mercifully put a mark on Cain. Sometimes we think of the "mark of Cain" as a curse put upon him by God. This was not the case at all. We are not told in Scripture precisely what the mark was or how people came to know its significance, but the mark, whatever it was, was a sign of God's grace toward Cain. It was intended to keep others from slaying him (Genesis 4:15). While it preserved his physical life, the sorry aftermath of all this was summed up in the tragic words, "And Cain went out from the presence of the Lord" (4:16). Many today, like Cain of old, set their path away from God, thinking this is the path of liberation when in reality it is the path of bondage and fear.

Cain typifies the unloving, the self-concerned, the jealous, the willful, the unrepentant, the brutal. It was not long before one of his descendants, Lamech, was bragging to his wives that he had slaughtered a man for merely bruising him (4:23, 24). How fast civilization was advancing!

Cain and Crisis

Where was the crisis for Cain? Was it when he failed to make an offering that was pleasing to God? Was it when he failed to heed God's correction? Was it when he was angry and crestfallen? Was it when he opened the door to hate? Was it when he invited his brother to go into the fields with him? Was it when he murderously shed the blood of his brother? Was it when he tried to stonewall it with God?

31

Wherever you place the decisive crisis, it is clear that Cain failed in each of his moments of decision. He failed because he concocted his own solutions instead of looking to God for real answers. Each solution of his own devising thrust him further into the spiral of sin. Yet God's grace continued to be extended to his life. Among his descendants was the violent Lamech (4:23), a man whose multiple marriages reflect his spiritual restlessness and whose song, the oldest recorded song in the world (Genesis 4:23, 24), boasted that he had killed a man and a youth who had done him injury. Vengeance was his pride and joy, as it has been for countless descendants of Cain from that time onward.

Among Cain and his descendants were city builders (Cain), nomads and herdsmen (Jabal), musicians (Jubal), and artisans and metalworkers (Tubal-cain). Among these people we have the originators of much of what we call civilization: city organization, domestication of animals, travel, metalworking, music, arts, and crafts. Ray Stedman writes thus:

> There is a picture of civilization: Technical brilliance producing comforts and luxuries; the substitution of the state for the family; the trend toward urban over rural life; the increasing toleration of sexual excess; and the passionate vindication of violence on the grounds of the protection of rights. Sound familiar? Human nature has not changed one iota in the ... years of history recorded since Cain.[1]

In due course, God provided another son for Adam and Eve, Seth. His name meant "appointed" because Eve said God had appointed him to take the place of Abel, the righteous son who had been murdered. Seth had a son whom he called Enos, "mortal," perhaps to recognize that life was fragile and continually dependent on the providence of God. It was at this time, we are told, that men and women began to call upon the name of the Lord (Genesis 4:26). There is nothing like our fragile mortality, our awareness of the presence of death in our genes and in our generations, to send us to our knees in prayer. See how Genesis 5 calls attention to death. Like a refrain is the phrase "and he died" (verses 5, 8, 11, 14, 17, 20, 27, 31). Only Enoch escaped (verse 24).

---

1. Ray C. Stedman, *The Beginnings,* copyright © 1978, p. 42; used by permission of Word Books, Publisher, Waco, Texas 76796.

Through Seth's line came Enoch (Genesis 5:18-24), a man noteworthy for his walk with God, for his departure to be with God, and for his prophecy of judgment (Jude 14, 15). He had a son whom he named Methuselah. This man lived to be 969 years old and he died in the very year that the flood came. God allowed this man to live longer than any other man has ever lived, perhaps to illustrate His compassion and longsuffering. Through this line, as we will soon learn, came Noah, the faithful servant of God. And it was through this line that Jesus the Redeemer eventually came (Luke 3:38).

The long lives of these pre-flood persons continue to be a puzzle to us. Do they, we wonder, reflect dramatic differences in the earth and its inhabitants before the flood? Despite this puzzle, the genealogy of chapter 5 illustrates the importance of walking with God, the longsuffering of God, and the inevitability of judgment on evil. These are great thoughts for today.

For Reflection

1. Read Genesis 4:1-4. What are some possible reasons that Abel's sacrifice was pleasing to God and Cain's was not? In what ways can our offerings to God be displeasing to Him?

2. What are the meanings of the names of the children of Adam and Eve? Why were those names given?

3. In what ways was Cain like his parents? In what ways was he like us? Are we guilty of blaming others for problems that are between ourselves and God?

4. What do we learn from this incident about our offerings to God?

5. What is the purpose of offerings to God?

6. How was God's patience with Cain demonstrated?

7. What good things in civilization are seen in Cain's descendants? What evil things?

8. Why do religious questions and observances often become the source of disobedience, dissension, hatred, and violence? What can keep them from becoming so?

9. Do you find it hard to understand why God allows good people to suffer at the hands of evil people? Can you give contemporary examples of this same thing?

10. If you could rewrite this story with a happy ending, how would you change it?

Perspectives on the Brotherhood Crisis

• Abel's blood cried for justice. The blood of Jesus calls for mercy. Thus the writer of Hebrews could write that Christians have come "to Jesus, the mediator of the new covenant, and to the blood of sprinkling, that speaketh better things than that of Abel" (Hebrews 12:24).

• Evil men and women cannot endure the sight of goodness in others around them.

• "If any one says, 'I love God,' and hates his brother, he is a liar; for he who does not love his brother whom he has seen, cannot love God whom he has not seen" (1 John 4:20, RSV).

4

Crisis
in Faith
Genesis 6—10

Thus far in our studies, man has not coped very well with crisis. Faced with high moments of decision, he has consistently chosen to go against the will of God. We have found few models to emulate in our own struggles, but we have seen a number of bad examples to warn us against the errors they made.

Things were going from bad to worse. The inner pollution of corruption was manifesting itself everywhere in the outward pollution of violence. "The earth also was corrupt before God; and the earth was filled with violence" (Genesis 6:11). Man, exalting himself as his only standard of good and evil, was sinking deeper and deeper into wickedness. It got so bad that "God saw that the wickedness of man was great in the earth, and that every imagination of the thoughts of his heart was only evil continually" (6:5). And God determined to bring an end to it all.

Here was a crisis of monumental proportions for the human race. And precisely at this moment of crisis we find a man of faith. "Noah found grace in the eyes of the Lord" (6:8).

What follows is not so much the story of a flood as it is the story of Noah and his family and their partnership with God in the preservation of the human race. There are four parts to the story. The first is an account of Noah's holiness and the wickedness of mankind (6:9-13). The second is an account of Noah's preservation (6:14—8:19).

The third is an account of God's covenant with Noah, the father of a new race (8:20—9:17). The fourth is an account of a happening between Noah and his sons that foreshadowed lasting dissension among Noah's descendants (9:18-29).

The Man of the Hour

What kind of a man was this who faced the coming doom of mankind with a hammer in his hand and words of love on his lips? (2 Peter 2:5). The Bible's description of him is brief but comprehensive.

Genesis 6:9 tells us that "Noah was a just man and perfect in his generations, and Noah walked with God." What a wonderful character sketch condensed into so few words! He was a righteous, perfect man in a violent environment.

Those things that God seeks in men and women were found in Noah. He conformed to God's high standards of excellence. If Noah was a beacon of righteousness, he was the more striking because of the moral darkness in which he shone (6:11-13). Though not necessarily morally perfect, Noah, like Enoch before him, walked with God (5:24; 6:9). What higher praise could be imagined? God removed Enoch from the world unto himself. By way of contrast, God removed the violent world from Noah, leaving this righteous man and his family to begin a new world.

Noah believed God. That belief caused him to spend over a hundred years (6:3) in a task that to everyone else must have seemed silly in the extreme. "By faith Noah, being warned of God of things not seen as yet, moved with fear, prepared an ark to the saving of his house; by the which he condemned the world, and became heir of the righteousness which is by faith" (Hebrews 11:7).

The Critical Task

We are not told whether or not Noah had any particular skill as a carpenter. If he knew little when he began his task, he certainly knew quite a lot more when he finished it.

It is significant that God and Noah were covenant-partners in the preservation of the human race. While God could have managed the cleansing of His earth in innumerable ways, He chose to accomplish it in partnership with a man of faith and his family. God made similar choices in many of His significant acts in human history, including the birth of the Redeemer and the proclamation of the gospel throughout the world.

36

God gave Noah the plan for the ark, but He did not give him a ready-made boat. God undoubtedly assisted in the assembling of the animals, but it was Noah who cared for them and who cut the beams and assembled the structure. It was Noah too who gathered the food for the year-long stay in the ark (6:21).

By any standard the ark was a large structure. Since its purpose was to float, not necessarily to sail, many scholars think it had the appearance of a box with three stories. While most of the exact details are not mentioned, we know that it had rooms, some sort of window, provision for ventilation around the top, and a door in its side. It was probably at least 450 feet long, 75 feet wide, and 45 feet high. Such a boat would have over a million and a half cubic feet, and the three stories would have a total deck area of more than a hundred thousand square feet. Scholars are uncertain of the material of its construction, but most identify gopher wood as being what we know as cypress. To make it watertight, the box was covered inside and out with pitch, an abundant substance in Mesopotamia.

It is easy to imagine the solitary, determined labor that went into the construction of this large structure. What faith it took to continue in the face of certain ridicule! Had Noah kept silent about his task, his neighbors might have interpreted his building as some monumental structure for conventional purposes. But Noah was not silent. He was a "preacher of righteousness" (2 Peter 2:5).

The Day of Reckoning

Things were going along as usual on the earth on the day that Noah and his family entered the ark. Babies were being born, young people were being married, women were baking at their ovens, men were working in the fields. There was nothing to indicate, at least for them, that this day was different from any other.

The ark was now finished. The birds and animals were safely stowed within, the clean beasts by sevens, the unclean by pairs, male and female. At the command of God, Noah and his wife, their three sons and their wives all entered the structure. Eight only! Eight people out of step with the world around them. Eight people who believed God's words waited in the ark seven days for the fulfillment of God's judgment. We can only wonder what went through their minds as the final countdown began and they realized that the world as they knew it would soon be no more.

Noah built the ark, but God shut the door (7:16). Men go along thinking they are getting away with wickedness, but there eventually comes a day when God steps into history and brings an end.

Noah was six hundred years old when the rains began to fall and the "fountains of the great deep" were broken up. The rain came for forty days and forty nights. Noah and his family were destined to remain in the ark for about a year. "And all flesh died that moved upon the earth, both of fowl, and of cattle, and of beast, and of every creeping thing that creepeth upon the earth, and every man ... and Noah only remained alive, and they that were with him in the ark" (7:21-23).

The Multicolored Sign of the Covenant

No sooner had Noah stepped out on dry land than he built an altar and made a sacrifice of praise to God. The sacrifice was pleasing to God. He pledged never again to interrupt so mightily the normal working of the world until its ultimate end. "While the earth remaineth, seedtime and harvest, and cold and heat, and summer and winter, and day and night shall not cease" (8:22).

As God had said to Adam and Eve at the dawn of creation, He now said to those through whom humanity had been saved: "Be fruitful, and multiply, and replenish the earth" (9:1). God's blessing included the assurance that all creatures on the earth and in the sea would be subject to man. These creatures would provide him with food. Out of deference for life, however, he was not to eat or drink the blood of animals. Further, in respect for the fact that man was created in God's image, murder was to be punished by taking the offender's life (9:2-7).

God made a solemn agreement with all living, breathing things. He would never again destroy the earth and its creatures with a flood. The rainbow was to be a sign of that promise. We do not know whether the rainbow was a new thing or whether it was an existing thing that was given a new meaning as a sign of God's promise. But now when a cloud came over the earth and the sun's rays caught it, the bow arched through the sky as a glorious reminder of God's covenant. Even God himself would be reminded by this visible phenomenon (9:16). It's not that God is forgetful, but with these words He underlined His own firm commitment to His unshakable promise.

Two Curious Events With Far-Reaching Results

Just before the account of Noah and the flood, we read in Genesis 6:2 that "the sons of God saw the daughters of men that they were fair; and they took them wives of all which they chose." Many scholars find this puzzling, and it has been interpreted in three different ways.

First, some have taken this to mean that angels, perhaps fallen angels, married human woman and produced a race of giants (verse 4). The phrase "sons of God" does seem to refer to angels in Job 1:6 and 2:1. However, Matthew 22:30 seems to indicate that angels are not designed for marriage, and "sons of God" does not necessarily mean angels. Human beings are called "children of the Most High" in Psalm 82:6 and "sons of the Living God" in Hosea 1:10. In the New Testament, those redeemed through Christ are called "sons of God" (John 1:12; Romans 8:14, 19; Philippians 2:15; 1 John 3:1, 2).

Second, some suppose that the "sons of God" in this verse are men of Seth's family, while the "daughters of men" are women of Cain's family. It is probably true that godliness lasted longer in Seth's family than in Cain's. Enoch was of Seth's line, and so was Noah. But can we believe that the family was so uniformly good that people were called "sons of God" simply because they were in that family?

Third, some think that "sons of God" in this instance means simply godly men. Attracted by physical beauty, some of them married women who were not so godly. As a result, the godly became less godly. Some of their sons and grandsons were "mighty men" (verse 4), powerful leaders in those violent days; but they became more and more wicked until goodness was almost lost (verse 5).

A second curious incident occurred after the flood. In time Noah planted a vineyard. After waiting a few years for it to bear fruit, he must have taken special pleasure in the first vintage of his garden. Drinking his wine, however, he became drunk and lay naked in his tent. It is hard for us to know whether Noah was reckless or merely ignorant. Had he been a drinker of water through all his life? Certainly he had never joined his neighbors in dissipation. Could this have been his first experience with anything intoxicating?

His son, Ham, observed his father in this inebriated, unclothed state and reported it to his brothers, Shem and Japheth. We are not told how he described it to his brothers, but the suggestion is that it was done in a leering, ridiculing way. His brothers, however, responded by respectfully covering their father (9:23).

When Noah learned what had happened, he pronounced blessing on the descendants of Shem and Japheth, and subservience on Ham's fourth son, Canaan. Ham's disrespect, Noah seemed to be saying, would break out especially in that branch of his family.

The prophecy proved to be true. In later centuries the descendants of Canaan became so depraved that God sent the Israelites to destroy them and take over their land. Canaanites who escaped death were made "hewers of wood and drawers of water" (Joshua 9:27). That is, they were required to do menial work for the Israelites. Each one became, as Noah had foretold, "a servant of servants."

Retrospect

If ever a man and his family were faced with critical decisions, Noah and his family were. Out of step with everyone but God, given a task that to most people seemed impossible and ridiculous, ignored by those he sought to save, Noah persevered in faith.

It was faith that sawed and hammered, lifted and hewed. It was faith that provided. It was faith that saved. It was faith that thanked. It was faithfulness that endured in difficult circumstances. See Hebrews 11:7.

Would that we ourselves could merit the summary statement applied to Noah: "According to all that God commanded him, so did he" (6:22).

For Reflection

1. How were Noah and his family different from the other people of their time?

2. Why was God so displeased with mankind?

3. What does the record of the flood tell us about God's attitude toward sin?

4. What did walking with God (Genesis 6:9) mean in the life of Noah?

5. What about the ark and its occupants or the flood itself is most fascinating to you personally?

6. If you would live in your generation as Noah did in his, how would your life be different from what it is now?

7. Why do you think Noah is often portrayed humorously in modern cartoons and jokes? How should a Christian react to that?

8. After the flood, what was God's promise to Noah and his descendants? (Genesis 8:21, 22).

9. Write the kind of prayer you think Noah would have uttered when he stepped out of the ark onto dry land.

10. What insights and lessons does the New Testament draw from Noah and the flood? See Matthew 24:37-44; Hebrews 11:7; 1 Peter 3:20, 21; 2 Peter 2:4-10.

Perspectives on the Faith Crisis

• God frequently works in partnership with faithful men and women to accomplish His saving work.

• It may seem that evil is going unpunished in the world, but eventually there comes a day of reckoning.

• The same flood that drowned the world floated the ark. Those outside the ark and those within faced the same circumstances, but faith provided a way of safety.

• "But as the days of Noah were, so shall also the coming of the Son of man be. For as in the days that were before the flood they were eating and drinking, marrying and giving in marriage, until the day that Noah entered into the ark, and knew not until the flood came, and took them all away; so shall also the coming of the Son of man be. . . . Watch therefore· for ye know not what hour your Lord doth come" (Matthew 24:37-42).

5

Crisis
in Trust
Genesis 11, 12

Sin in the Garden of Eden brought at least three significant separations—separation between man and God, separation between man and man, and separation between man and his environment. Cain's murder of his brother manifested the violence that came into human affairs. But Noah's saving faith started things anew.

Before long, however, man's pride, arrogance, and obstinacy became so apparent that God intervened to bring about another separation. Language, rather than uniting men as it had from the beginning, became the divider of men (Genesis 11:9).

From the beginning of human time, there had been one language among all people. Today we long for a return to such a situation. Though various attempts have been made to find or create a language that all can use, these attempts have failed. We are plagued with the difficulties that the diverse languages of the world create—misunderstanding, suspicion, fear, distrust, separation, alienation, difficulty of communication, to name only a few. This sorry condition of mankind traces its origin to the descendants of Noah who settled in the plain of Shinar and began to build there a great brick city and tower to glorify themselves (11:1-4). They had developed the ability to construct magnificent buildings with burned brick for their construction material and bitumen for their mortar. Their excitement with their growing numbers and ability made them self-centered and arrogant. They felt that nothing was beyond them, even a tower that would reach to heaven. Their goal was to bind their people together around their magnificent creations and the greatness of their reputation. Predominant was a desire and to "make a name" for themselves.

There has always been a great temptation for man to define himself by the things he can make, discover, manipulate, own, look at, and control. At its heart, this is the temptation to look for unity, significance, and immortality in human accomplishments, not in God. The haughty goal of the people of Babel was unity for their own glory, buildings for their own glory, and unlimited accomplishment for their own glory. However, their selfish desire for glory was thwarted when God confounded their language and thus scattered them from that place. The separation they feared was brought about because of their arrogant trust in their own accomplishments rather than faithful trust in God. Like many of us, they sought greatness in their ingenuity rather than in their walk with God. As our technology threatens to do, their accomplishments led to their downfall. Through several centuries the scattered families kept moving out to more distant places.

Then God began, through a chosen and faithful human being, the long process of man's rehabilitation and reconciliation that was to be completed in Jesus Christ. As he had done with Noah, God once again entered into a special covenant with a faithful man, Abram.

The Call

God said to a man living in lower Mesopotamia, "Get thee out of thy country, and from thy kindred, and from thy father's house, unto a land that I will show thee" (12:1). It is hard to see in this command much movement toward the one who would crush the serpent's head (3:15), but the command was one large step in that direction. The man God called was Abram, later named Abraham.

Abram faced a moment of decision. It is possible that he was a well-established businessman in Ur. Albright, a prominent Old Testament scholar, believed that Abram was a wealthy trader, a leading figure in the donkey caravan business that moved goods throughout the Fertile Crescent. From every normal point of view, God's command seemed risky at best.

Abram stood at the crossroads. Like many a man since, he was faced with a decision concerning God's will for his life. It was clear to him what God wanted: he was to go to some other land. But his problem was greater because God did not then tell him exactly where. Had he known, his decision might have been easier. Had God said to go to Canaan or to Egypt, then his actions might have seemed more rational to his family. "Where are you going?" his kindred must have asked as he packed his belongings and prepared to journey. "I don't know," he must have been forced to reply. "All I know is that God has told me to go and that He has told me He will lead me."

There must have been considerable head and beard scratching over Abram. But "Abraham believed God, and it was counted unto him for righteousness" (Romans 4:3; Galatians 3:6).

The Contract

God did not ask Abram to do something without promising him something. His descendants would multiply until they became a great nation. His name would be exalted. He would be spoken of with high honor. He would be uniquely God's man. Those who opposed him could expect God's opposition. Those who showed him kindness could expect God's blessing. And finally, the whole human creation would be blessed through him (12:2, 3; 13:14-17; 17:3-8; 22:15-18). This promise of blessing to all nations was remarkably fulfilled in Jesus, a descendant of Abram who brought redemption to *all* people who would accept it (Galatians 3:8, 9; Acts 3:25, 26). God's Son restored unity to an alienated and divided world.

Perhaps in light of the promises involved and understanding the full story as we now do, it is difficult for us to see this moment as a time of major crisis for Abram. Yet those of us who have traveled, who have been strangers in foreign lands, and who have been outsiders, may appreciate some of the thoughts that must have gone through Abram's mind.

The Commandment

A new age was dawning as he began his exodus. As he moved away from the walls of Ur, heading north with his considerable retinue, he could scarcely have realized what chain of events he was setting in motion by his act of simple faith.

His first long stop was a caravan city to the north, Haran. There he dwelt for some time and seems to have greatly prospered. But at the age of seventy-five he resumed his journey toward Canaan (11:31— 12:5; Acts 7:2-4).

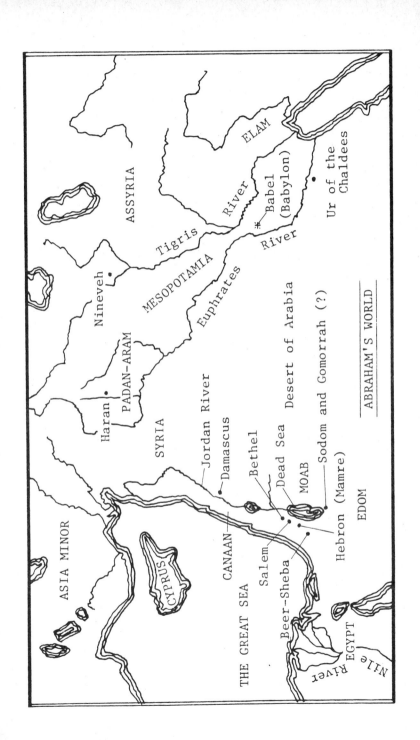

ABRAHAM'S WORLD

In Canaan, God promised that the land he was passing through as a traveler would one day be the home of the nation that would call him father (12:6-9). Abram was in constant communion with God. In an act reminiscent of his ancestor Noah's first act after the flood, Abram built an altar unto the Lord.

The Crisis

Abram, for all his simple trust, had his own lessons to learn. A natural crisis became God's instrument of instruction. Abram had left a well-watered and fertile land. Suddenly he found himself in the midst of famine. The Bible says that the famine was grievous. We can only imagine the dried-up watercourses and the dusty well bottoms, the dwindling flocks, and the scorching sun that Abram and his large party found as they moved toward the south. Sun, thirst, death—three reminders of man's dependence on the providence of God. Abram was learning that even in a promised land, food and clothing and life itself must come from the Lord.

The Contrivance

Abram headed for Egypt, where the mighty Nile made famine very rare. There the civilization matched or surpassed that of Abram's old home on the Euphrates. The pyramids were already six or seven hundred years old.

As the caravan approached this sophisticated land, Abram's faith began to waver. God had said He would bless whoever blessed Abram and curse whoever cursed him. The promise surely applied to his wife and family as well, but Abram was not going to take any chances. Like many of us since, he applied human deception and crafty duplicity to a situation that demanded only straightforward faith and trust.

Sarai, Abram's wife, was quite good-looking. She was then about sixty-five (middle-age, since she lived to 127), and Abram was not sure he could trust the Egyptians.

If ever there was a mixed compliment, it was Abram's words to his wife. He started out with words dear to any woman's heart: "I know that thou art a fair woman to look upon." That surely brought a smile to her lovely lips. But what he said then must have furrowed her brow: "Say, I pray thee, thou art my sister: that it may be well with me for thy sake; and my soul shall live because of thee" (12:11-13). It seems that his compliment was related to a desire to save his own life (12:12).

If anything can be said in Abram's defense, it is that it is unfair to judge him by the standards of our time and place rather than his. Probably no one in Chaldea or Canaan or Egypt would consider his strategem as despicable as it seems to us. But mistreatment of his wife is not the only thing Abram may be blamed for. The fact that he felt the need of such a plan suggests a failure of his trust in God.

God had promised Abram that he would be the father of a nation. His death before having a child, therefore, was highly unlikely. God had told him that he would be on his side in any confrontation with others (12:3). But Abram took things into his own hands—and really fouled them up.

What Abram said was not a total lie. Sarai really was his half-sister (20:12). But no amount of rationalization could excuse his faltering trust, as he soon learned.

In Egypt, Abram's duplicity caught up with him. His caravan was impressive enough for the princes of Pharaoh to notice it. But it was Sarai, his "sister," who really caught their eye. Always on the lookout for something new to beautify the house of Pharaoh, the king's agents praised her beauty before the king.

We can only imagine Abram's feelings on the day Pharaoh's beauty scouts picked up his "sister" and transported her to the house of the king. If Abram was upset by what his lie brought about, he could at least congratulate himself because he had not been killed. Besides, his feelings may have been somewhat mitigated by the stream of royal gifts that began appearing at his tent because of Sarai (12:16). Of course it would be an insult to the king to return the gifts, and perhaps Abram felt that the sheep, the oxen, the asses, the servants, and the camels were not a bad antidote for the loss of a wife, even a beautiful one.

If Abram was getting the impression that deceiving men and doubting God could be profitable, he was soon to be set straight.

The Confrontation

We know little about the plagues that came upon Pharaoh and his house (12:17). Somehow he learned that Sarai was Abram's wife and that he was being plagued because he had taken her. Pharaoh was angry, to say the least. When Abram stood before him, the king dressed him down: "What have you done to me? Why didn't you tell me she was your wife?" (12:18, 19). Abram, humbled, could not utter a word in his defense.

47

Pharaoh canceled Abram's visa and booted (or should we say "sandaled") him out of the country (12:19). Had the king not been aware of God's presence with this scheming man, he might have punished Abram more severely. He might even have taken Abram's life—the very thing the ruse had been designed to prevent. As it was, Pharaoh saw to it that Abram was escorted to the border (12:20).

Abram had prospered in Egypt. He had cattle and silver and gold (13:2). But perhaps the greatest benefit received from the sojourn was a renewed resolution to trust in the providence of God.

As Abram sat once again by the altar he had built in Canaan, his mind must have gone over the events of the years since he had left Ur. As he looked at the flocks and possessions, he may have thought of his narrow escape in Egypt and been thankful for God's sustaining grace. Sitting by that altar, as yet without a son by that beautiful and coveted wife, he must have wondered what God yet had in store for him.

For Reflection

1. What did the inhabitants of Babel hope to accomplish by their building activity? What is ironic about their purpose and the result?

2. In what ways today do people and nations try to make a name for themselves?

3. In what ways does language present a barrier to man's ambitions? Do you see this as good or as bad for man?

4. What was God's command to Abram? (12:1). What were His promises? (12:2,3).

5. Of Abram's actions recorded in Genesis 12, which demonstrated faith and which did not?

6. Compose a prayer that Abram might have uttered before his going into Egypt. Compose another prayer that he might have offered after his experience in Egypt.

7. How do you think Sarai felt about what befell in Egypt?

8. What things made it difficult for Abram to follow God's commands? What things make it difficult for us to follow and trust God?

9. How can it be said that the world has been blessed through Abraham?

10. What does it mean to you that "Abraham believed God, and it was reckoned to him for righteousness"? (Romans 4:3; Galatians 3:6).

Perspectives on the Trust Crisis

- Sometimes launching out in faith means leaving security behind.
- Even the faithful sometimes become enamored with their own schemes to the point of relying on themselves rather than the promises of God.
- Decisive trust in God brings benefits that ripple outward and onward from our lives.
- "By faith Abraham obeyed when he was called to go out to a place which he was to receive as an inheritance; and he went out, not knowing where he was to go" (Hebrews 11:8, RSV).

6

Crisis
in Doubt
Genesis 13–17

With the call of Abram, God began working out His redemptive purposes through a nation. The importance of Abram can easily be seen in the book of Genesis. Eleven chapters are given over to the thousands of years preceding him (Genesis 1—11). Fourteen chapters tell the history of Abram and his immediate family (12—25). The remaining twenty-five chapters of Genesis are given to three generations: Isaac, Jacob, and Joseph (26—50). It is easy to see that the pace of the historical narrative slowed down considerably in telling of Abram. In the chapters ahead of us we will study some remarkable events in the life of this unusual family.

The Problems of Wealth
Abram returned from Egypt a wealthy man (13:1-5). Prosperity frequently brings its own problems. Some of us like to think wealth can remove all our difficulties, but that is not generally the case. It was certainly not the case with Abram. No sooner had he settled back in Bethel than his herdsmen and those of Lot, his nephew, began a dispute over grazing land. Possessions came between two men who shared both faith and family ties. The Bible says, "For their substance was great, so that they could not dwell together" (13:6). How frequently throughout history material possessions have broken unity and divided families!

Abram approached this prosperity problem peacefully and unselfishly, not seeking his own gain. He rightfully deserved first choice of the land, but he gave that choice to Lot in order to avoid strife and bitterness (13:7-9). For all his costly acquisitions, Abram had not acquired an acquisitive spirit. He was content to rely on God's promises to bless him.

Lot, however, seems to have developed a different spirit. There is more than a little hint of greed in his choice of the well-watered plain of Jordan. He was going to look out for himself. But while looking out for number one in respect to his cattle and flocks, he made a tragic error in regard to his own soul.

The Jordan valley was extremely fertile. It could be compared with the Garden of Eden or the lush valley of the Nile (13:10). But a certain ominous ring sounds with the words that close this incident. Lot "pitched his tent toward Sodom" (13:11, 12).

Before long Lot was living *in* Sodom, a city of exceeding wickedness (13:13). He was able to maintain his own righteousness, but he was soon to learn the cost of closing his eyes to his sinful environment in order to achieve private gain. Abram, by way of contrast, confirmed once again in the promises of God, moved to Hebron (13:14-18).

Abram to the Rescue

We might not be surprised if we found that Abram had developed a taste of bitterness toward Lot for his quick land grab at their last meeting. We might have expected Abram to say, "Serves him right," when one of Lot's servants came running into Abram's camp with bad news. Lot and his household had become embroiled in a rebellion by a number of local princes against Chedorlaomer, king of Elam. Lot had been taken captive (14:1-13).

With the speed of a born swashbuckler, Abram sprang into action. Quickly he armed over three hundred men and dashed north. Abram knew his guerrilla warfare. Surprise and speed were his allies, as well as God, as he whisked Lot away from his captors. The expedition was so successful that he not only rescued Lot, but also liberated women, servants, and all the possessions that had been taken from a wide area near Sodom (14:14-17).

How thankful Lot must have been toward his enterprising uncle! But if Lot ever thought of rewarding him by giving up some of his lush pasturage, we are not told of it. Lot was vexed with wicked Sodom (2 Peter 2:7), but not enough to leave town.

On their joyous return, Abram met the king of Salem, Melchizedek, who was a priest of God. Melchizedek properly praised God for Abram's success, and Abram responded by giving him tithes (14:18-20). This Melchizedek, who appears in the narrative with no mention of his ancestry, became a type of Jesus' high priesthood (Hebrews 5:5, 6; 6:20; 7:1-28).

The Reward

The king of Sodom, grateful to Abram for the liberation of his hijacked possessions and kidnapped subjects, offered Abram the battle spoils as a reward for his quick and decisive action (14:21). Abram, however, had no desire to be in any way subject to the king of Sodom or to profit from the loss of others. He was content to rely on God's promises to provide for him. He wanted to be in debt to no man, least of all the king of such a city as Sodom (14:22-24).

Abram had met two crises well. He had come to the aid of his nephew with courage; he had rescued Lot with no resentment for his nephew's selfishness in the matter of the division of the land. Further, Abram rejected the temptation to become debtor to a corrupt establishment or to become rich at the expense of others. He was learning a great deal about relying on God.

A Family Failure

When God next spoke to Abram of His promises, Abram pointed out that as yet he had no child (15:1-3). Abram's questioning spirit should have been satisfied when God assured him that his own true son would fulfill God's promise (15:4). God took Abram out into the dark night and showed him the stars of the heavens. "Look now toward heaven, and tell the stars, if thou be able to number them: and he said unto him, So shall thy seed be" (15:5).

Abram "believed in the Lord; and he counted it to him for righteousness" (15:6). After Abram had made an offering he fell into a deep sleep in which God revealed to him in precise detail what lay ahead for his descendants (15:7-21).

If Abram was content to wait for God to fulfill His promises in His own good time, his wife Sarai was not so patient. Abram was now in his eighties, and she was in her seventies. Sarai felt they could wait no longer. They had to take things into their own hands. Perhaps, she thought, God needs assistance.

Sarai urged Abram to have a child by her Egyptian servant girl, Hagar. From a human standpoint this made sense. It was apparently a common custom of the day, and it would serve to produce the desired heir.

Abram listened to Sarai's urgings, though her plan implied doubt of God's fulfillment of His promise. But then, after all, Abram *would* be the father—and the line would get started—and wasn't that what God wanted? So Abram slept with Hagar, and before long she was pregnant (16:1-4a).

Hagar was well pleased with herself, but her pleasure turned to pride. Perhaps she began to see the coming child as an opportunity to supplant her mistress in the eyes of Abram. The Bible says "her mistress was despised in her eyes" (16:4). This became intolerable for Sarai. A showdown was inevitable.

Perhaps in tears, Sarai appealed to Abram, who took her side in the matter. Bolstered by his support, Sarai repaid Hagar with cruelty until the poor pregnant girl ran away (16:4b-6).

Half a century of marriage without children made Sarai doubt that God's promise could ever be fulfilled through her. Doubt led to a human solution for a situation that demanded simple reliance on God. The human solution led to family squabble and alienation. Yet God intervened even then to show His love for Abram and his descendants. The angel of the Lord found Hagar on her way to Egypt. He sent her back to Abram's household with a promise that her son, though unruly, would be the father of an uncounted multitude (16:7-16). We know his descendants as the Arabs.

The Token of the Covenant

Time passed. Abram was ninety-nine years old. More than a quarter of a century had elapsed since he had left Ur at God's command. Sarai had now passed beyond the point where women talk about their age. She and her husband were at home in the promised land; but with regard to a whole nation of descendants, all they had were promises (12:1-3, 7; 13:14-17; 15:18-21). Abram certainly knew the promises *by heart,* even if he didn't always act as if he took them *to heart.* But God was moving toward the fulfillment of His purposes, whether Abram knew it or not. He spoke once again, calling upon Abram to be complete, perfect, upright, righteous, and unfaltering. Again He promised those multitudes of descendants. Abram would be the father of many nations. He would father kings. (Among his descendants were kings like David and Solomon, but the greatest was the King of kings, even Jesus.) If all of this sounds repetitious, it is. The repetition serves to emphasize this covenant.

The fulfillment of the promise lay in the future, but it was just as certain as if it had already happened. As a sign, God changed Abram's name, "exalted father," to Abraham, "father of a multitude." We wonder if there was a little mirth in the camp at Abram's expense when this childless "father of a multitude" began using his new name. Sarai also was given a new name. Sarai, "she who strives," became Sarah, "princess." Remember that she was pushing ninety when she received this new name. Her acceptance of the name implied faith on her part that God would fulfill His promise to make her the mother of kings and nations (17:1-8, 15, 16).

In the rainbow, God had given Noah a visible sign of His covenant. Now God designated a visible sign of His covenant with Abraham. It was circumcision (17:9-14, 23-27). This became the mark of God's possession of the descendants of Abraham. Ray Stedman writes, "It was placed upon this particular part of the body to indicate that they were to be physically separate from the other nations. The very organ by which that separation could be violated, bore upon it the mark of God's ownership."[1] According to the New Covenant, circumcision is not of the body but of the heart (Romans 2:28, 29). Christians bear the mark of God's possession on their mind, will, emotions.

Not the Last Laugh

In the midst of this solemn talk of kings, nations, names, and covenants, Abraham fell on his face and laughed (17:15-17).

Was it an incredulous laugh of joy at the remarkable things that most certainly were to come? Or was it the scornful laugh of an unbelieving Abraham who was, as it were, saying to the Lord, "You've got to be kidding"? We can't be sure.

The context gives little help. Ishmael was thirteen years old. If Abraham was laughing for joy over the promise of blessing for his line through Sarah, his mention of Ishmael may have been a loving father's request that Hagar's son also figure in some way in the blessing. If Abraham's laugh was a laugh of doubt, then he may have been suggesting that Ishmael could well be the one to father the promised nation.

Whatever Abraham was thinking, God assured him that the promise would be fulfilled through his son by Sarah (17:19-22). Now for

---

1. Ray C. Stedman, "The Circumcised Life," *Discovery Paper,* No. 3664., © 1968. Used by permission of Discovery Publishing, Palo Alto, California.

the first time, God set the actual date. Sarah would have a baby the next year (17:21). A quarter of a century after she and Abram left Haran, the waiting would be over.

For Reflection

1. In what ways does Abram demonstrate greatness in the events recorded in Genesis 13—17?

2. In what instances does it appear that he was less a man of faith than he should have been?

3. What is the meaning of Genesis 15:13, 14? When was this prophecy fulfilled?

4. What mistake led to dissension in Abram's family?

5. How did Abram neglect his responsibilities in this family squabble?

6. What were God's promises and predictions concerning Hagar's son, Ishmael? What group of people today are the descendants of Ishmael?

7. What were the meanings of the new names given to Abram and Sarai? How did they fit with God's plans for them?

8. In what circumstances have you found that you must wait upon and trust in God?

9. Why do you think God's promises are sometimes delayed in their fulfillment? How does He reassure believers during these seeming delays?

10. What warning signals do we have in our lives when we are trying to do by our ingenuity things we should leave in the hands of God?

Perspectives on the Doubt Crisis

- Faith is both launching out and hanging in there.
- Sometimes our actions seem to contradict our faith.
- God sometimes chooses to make His mighty power known through the unexpected.
- To wait is sometimes as great an act of faith as to act.

7

Crisis
in Obedience
Genesis 18–22

Hospitality is one of the prized characteristics of the Middle Eastern gentleman today, even as it was in Abraham's day. When Abraham saw three strangers passing by, he urged them to stop for a rest beneath the tree that shaded his tent at Mamre.

Unexpected guests, so dear to the open-hearted husband, can be a pain to a hard-working wife. There was a great hustle and bustle as Sarah slaved over the hot hearth to bake bread and as Abraham made ready a young calf. It was with justifiable pride that he at length stood back and watched his guests enjoying his quickly assembled banquet (18:1-8).

Sarah's Incredulous Laughter

The purpose of the visit of these three men finally became evident. For all their pleasure in talking man's talk with the head of this household, their visit was as much related to the owner of those flour-covered hands in Abraham's tent as it was to Abraham himself. One of the men declared that Sarah would have a son before the next year would pass. Sarah, eavesdropping at the tent flap, laughed.

Not long before, Abraham had laughed at the same news (17:15-18). We are not sure whether he laughed in joy or in disbelief and scorn, but it seems that Sarah's laugh was a scornful laugh of unbelief: "Hmph! I should live so long! A child? These fellows have a weird sense of humor." Their retort caught her in mid-laughter: "Is any thing too hard for the Lord?"

It soon became apparent to both Abraham and Sarah that these men were no ordinary visitors. Apparently they were angels (19:1). One of them in particular spoke as the voice of the Lord (18:13, 17). When he chided Sarah for her mocking of his promise, she gulped and said, "Who, me? Laugh? Not me!" Those flour-caked hands were shaking a little, not from old age, but from fear (18:13-15).

There may have been a lot of laughing in Abraham's camp about God's promises. But to God it was very serious business indeed. At stake here were God's word, God's covenant, God's plan for a chosen people, and God's plan for the redemption of mankind.

The Depravity of Sodom

As the visitors arose to leave, another very serious matter came into the conversation. These celestial beings were, it seemed, on a fact-finding trip to Sodom and Gomorrah (18:16-22).

Abraham already knew enough facts about those two cesspool cities to have little doubt that God's judgment on them was warranted. The other two angels went on toward Sodom, while Abraham continued to talk with the angel of God who remained to talk with him, the one who spoke as "the Lord."

Abraham had been told that the angels were there to assess the wickedness of Sodom and Gomorrah. Abraham knew of their wickedness, but he knew also that Sodom was the abode of his nephew, Lot. Perhaps he was thinking of his nephew's family when he said, "Wilt thou also destroy the righteous with the wicked?" (18:23). What followed sounds like an auction in reverse.

"If there are fifty, will you destroy it, Lord?"

"No."

"How about forty-five?"

"No."

"Forty?"

"No."

"Thirty?"

"No."

"Twenty?"

"No."

"Ten?"

"No."

Those familiar with Middle Eastern haggling may find this more than a little amusing. It would be much more amusing, however, if the situation in Sodom and Gomorrah had been less tragic. In those cities, not even ten righteous persons could be found (18:24-33).

Abraham appealed to God's justice, and God listened to him. We can learn something from Abraham's intercessory prayer. This incident illustrates the power of the prayers of the faithful as they relate to God's actions. (See Luke 11:5-13.) Delitzsch noted that such power would be impossible if God had not chosen to make it possible.

> This would indeed be neither permissible nor possible, had not God ... placed Himself in such a relation to men, that He not merely works upon them by means of His grace, but allows them to work upon Him by means of their faith; had He not interwoven the life of the free creature into His own absolute life, and accorded to a created personality the right to assert itself in faith, in distinction from His own.[1]

Lot's Lot

When the two angels in human form arrived at Sodom, they didn't have to inquire long to find Lot. There he was in the thick of things at the gate of the city. City gates in ancient times were places for business and socializing. Lot's presence there speaks much of his involvement in the life of that wicked city.

Lot proved to be as big-hearted a host as his uncle. The men intended to spend the night in the streets. Their purpose, as we remember, was fact-finding. Nevertheless, at Lot's urging, they came to his house (19:1-3).

Soon a mob gathered in Lot's front yard, demanding that these strangers be brought out so that they could be abused sexually. Poor Lot was in a quandary. He had a sacred duty of hospitality, for these men had come under the shadow of his roof (19:8). Custom demanded that he protect his guests with his life.

Lot had a crisis of some magnitude on his hands. He met it by a strange move. He sought to avoid sin by sinning. Not willing to sacrifice his duty as a host, he sacrificed his duty as a father. He

---

1. Taken from *Biblical Commentary on the Old Testament,* by Keil and Delitzsch. Used by permission of Wm. B. Eerdmans, Grand Rapids, Michigan.

offered his two virgin daughters to the crowd (19:8). Obviously Lot had been at home in Sodom much too long.

We are told in the New Testament that Lot was in acute mental distress because of the filthy lives of the godless people about him. He had suffered spiritual agonies day after day at what he had seen and heard (2 Peter 2:7, 8). But he had not moved out.

The citizens of the city were not about to have this outsider, Lot, tell them what they could or could not do. They shoved Lot aside and battered at the door. Then the angels intervened, striking the morally blind with physical blindness so they could no longer find the door (19:9-11).

The facts on Sodom were in. God's judgment would soon follow. The angels urged Lot to warn quickly any of his family that were in the wicked city. Lot hastened to find his sons-in-law. These were men to whom his daughters were engaged, or else men to whom other daughters were already married. Lot's urgent message of doom sounded to them like the ravings of a crazy man (19:12-14).

Whatever Lot had said to the Sodomites before, he now talked more urgently of sin, judgment, death, and salvation. But nobody would take him seriously, not even the young men he had deemed worthy to marry his daughters.

Even Lot seemed reluctant to leave the condemned city. He "lingered" until his celestial companions were forced to drag him and his family out of the gates of Sodom, "the Lord being merciful to him" (19:15, 16).

Had Lot become so softened by city living that he could no longer stand the independent life of the country? Despite the urging of the angels that he flee, he still desired to stay as near as possible to his old haunts (19:17-22). Lot no longer seemed capable of moving out on faith as he and Abraham had done before his years of ease in Sodom. He and his wife were to become proverbial as examples of those who are lured and lulled by sin.

Sodom and Gomorrah were utterly annihilated (19:23-28). Fire and brimstone rained down upon them, and "the smoke of the country went up as the smoke of a furnace." Many believe that the southern part of the Dead Sea today occupies the place where these sinful cities once stood, but they were destroyed so completely that not one stone can be identified as belonging to them.

Even though Lot escaped, the days in Sodom had taken their toll. He was a fear-ridden man (19:29, 30). Like an animal, he went to live in a cave. His daughters were little comfort to him. They had no faith in God to provide for them, no faith in their father to find them suitable husbands, and no faith in themselves to be desirable. So they made their father drunk and committed incest with him (19:31-38). They were true daughters of Sodom.

Lot is never mentioned again in the Genesis record. The events of Sodom became a permanent memory of the punitive righteousness of God. They should be kept constantly in mind, particularly as they illustrate God's certain judgment (Luke 17:28-37).

Abraham, the Slow Learner

One more failure of faith is recorded in Genesis before the birth of Abraham's long-awaited son. As he had done before in Egypt, Abraham told a half-lie about his wife, this time to Abimelech, king of Gerar. Sarah was now about ninety years old, so it was perhaps more diplomacy than desire that moved this Philistine king to take her into his harem (20:1, 2). This innocent act brought great distress into the house of Abimelech (20:17, 18), though he was kept, by the providence of God, from coming near Sarah. God once again came to Abraham and Sarah's rescue, though they scarcely deserved it (20:3-13). Abimelech even went so far as to shower gifts on Abraham when Sarah was returned to him (20:14-16). Abraham, like so many followers of God since, was blessed by the grace of God.

Laughter at Last

There was much laughter in the camp on the day that Sarah delivered her long-awaited firstborn. It was no longer the laughter of unbelief and dismay, but the joyous laughter of amazement at the marvelous works of God. We can almost hear Sarah's joy cascading down through the centuries: "God has brought me laughter! All who hear about this shall rejoice with me. For who would have dreamed that I would ever have a baby? Yet I have given Abraham a child in his old age!" (21:6, 7, LB). And they called the child Isaac, "laughter" (21:1-7).

There was another kind of laughter in the camp a few years later, however. It was not the laughter of joy, but of derision (21:8, 9). Ishmael was now in his teens and should have known better. Isaac was weaned, and a happy feast celebrated that milestone. Ishmael saw his parents' happiness. He remembered the joyous laughter that accompanied Isaac's birth. Undoubtedly he knew the divine promises connected with this small boy. As he made fun of this child of promise, Ishmael's laughter, filled with jealousy, bitterness, and ridicule, became a caricature of his parents' laughter of joy. In his envy he was not only mocking the child; he was also mocking God, who had named Isaac the child of promise.

Sarah insisted that Hagar and her son be sent away (21:10). We can imagine Abraham's anguish (21:11). This issue had been trouble in the camp for a long time, ever since he and Sarah had taken things into their own hands and tried to hasten the fulfillment of God's promises (Genesis 16).

Abraham had no desire to see his teenage son depart. Yet God chose this moment to renew His promise that through Isaac's line Abraham's descendants were to be called. Ishmael was to be blessed because he was a son of Abraham. He too would father a nation, but separation from the family of Abraham was called for (21:12, 13). So Hagar took her son and some provisions and headed into the wilderness, going in the direction of her own homeland, Egypt. God intervened to help and sustain her at a critical moment of need (21:14-20). The story of this tragic family breakup comes to an end on a positive note—Hagar found Ishmael a wife from the land of Egypt (21:21).

This incident was used by Paul to illustrate the Christian's freedom from bondage to the law.

> You and I, dear brothers, are the children that God prom-ised, just as Isaac was. And so we who are born of the Holy Spirit are persecuted now by those who want us to keep the Jewish laws, just as Isaac the child of promise was persecuted by Ishmael the slave-wife's son. But the Scriptures say that God told Abraham to send away the slave-wife and her son, for the slave-wife's son could not inherit Abraham's home and lands along with the free woman's son. Dear brothers, we are not slave children, obligated to the Jewish laws, but children of the free woman, acceptable to God because of our faith.
> —Galatians 4:28-31, LB.

Abraham's Test

Abraham made a serious mistake when he pretended that his wife was only his sister, but usually he dealt wisely and honorably with the people of the land he lived in, particularly with Abimelech (21:22-34). We are reminded of Abraham's faith as, at Beer-sheba, he continued that which had become his practice, the prayerful act of calling on the name of the Lord (21:33).

Sarah and Abraham saw the child of their old age grow. Now he was the one and only child, and they must have smothered him with attention. Before Isaac's birth, Sarah and Abraham may have had a tendency to think that if worse came to worst, God would work His promises through Ishmael. Now, however, Ishmael was gone. All depended on Isaac, the son of laughter. There must have been a lot of joy in the camp as the boy grew older.

Then there came a command from God that must have seemed inexplicable to Abraham (22:1, 2). In Ur, he had been instructed to set out on a journey of faith, not knowing where God would lead him. Now he was to set out on another journey of faith into Moriah, to a mountain that God would show him. He was to take his son, who was perhaps by now in his teens.

In Moriah he was to offer his son, the only son he now had, the son of promise, his beloved son, as a burnt offering. If Abraham discussed God's command with Sarah, we are not told of it. Holding his perplexity and grief within himself, Abraham cut wood and prepared for the journey (22:3).

For three days Abraham, his son, and the two young men who accompanied them journeyed north. What did they talk about? How did they pass the time as they sat in the evening by the fire? What thoughts went through Abraham's mind as he wrestled with the seeming contradiction of both morality and reason that God's command represented? Yet he went resolutely on.

Finally they were near the place. The young men and the donkey were left behind. Isaac shouldered the wood that had been brought. (It seems almost as if what was about to happen was too personal for even the donkey to witness.) Abraham took a knife and some hot coals in a pot, and the two, father and son, climbed together toward Mount Moriah (22:4-6).

There is deep pathos in the innocent question of the lad Isaac as they climbed upward: "Behold the fire and the wood: but where is the lamb for a burnt offering?" There is tenderness and more truth than he knew in Abraham's loving and evasive answer: "My son, God will provide . . ." (22:7, 8).

Both of them must have worked together to pick up the rough stones they heaped up to make an altar. What was Abraham thinking as they worked?

The wood was put in place. There was no turning back. Abraham called his bright-faced son of laughter to him and began to bind his hands and feet (22:9). Isaac then knew the answer to his question.

He did not struggle, whine, or run away. He allowed himself to be bound and placed on the altar. His own faith seems no less striking than that of his father.

Then Abraham took up the knife. . . .

The trial was over. The angel of the Lord stayed his hand, saying, "For now I know that thou fearest God, seeing thou hast not withheld thy son, thine only son, from me" (22:10-12).

God did provide the needed sacrifice in the form of a ram entangled in a nearby thicket. There must have been tears in Abraham's aging eyes as he, with the help of his son, extricated the ram and offered it to God (22:13, 14). Then from Heaven came the glorious blessing once again—God's swearing by himself to prosper this man who had not withheld from Him his only son (22:15-18).

We cannot read this story without hearing within it echoes of God's own sacrifice of His only begotten Son, Jesus. Mount Moriah came to be the place where the temple with all its sacrificial system stood (2 Chronicles 3:1). But only in the substitutionary death of Jesus did even that have meaning. The writer to the Hebrews sums all this up beautifully:

> It was by faith that Abraham, when put to the test, made a sacrifice of Isaac. Yes, the man who had heard God's promises was prepared to offer up his only son, of whom it had been said, "In Isaac shall thy seed be called." He believed that God could raise his son up, even if he were dead. And he did, in a manner of speaking, receive him back from death.
> —Hebrews 11:17-19, Phil.

For Reflection

1. Do you, like Sarah, ever act as if you thought something might be too hard for God? (18:9-14). What ought you to do in such instances?

2. What mistake of Abraham was rebuked in Egypt and yet repeated in another place more than twenty years later? (12:10-20; 20:1-18). What excuse did Abraham offer? What fears in your own life tempt you to distrust God?

3. Abraham deceived Abimelech, but afterward prayed for him (20:2, 17). What kind of relationship did the two have at a later time? (21:22-34).

4. How old were Abraham and Sarah when Isaac was born? (17:17; 21:5). Why was Isaac's name appropriate? (17:15-19; 18:10-15; 21:6, 7).

5. Why were Hagar and Ishmael sent away from Abraham's family? (21:9-21). Who was responsible for this? Explain Paul's allegorical interpretation of this event (Galatians 4:22—5:1).

6. What does it mean that God "tempted" Abraham? (22:1). What was Abraham commanded to do, as recorded in Genesis 22? What dilemma did that pose for him?

7. Review Abraham's history from chapters 12—22 of Genesis. Make a list of things he did that showed strong faith in God, and another list of things that showed faltering faith. Can you recall times when your faith has been strong, and other times when it has faltered?

8. What parallels do you see between the story of Abraham and Isaac and the New Testament record of the sacrifice of Jesus?

9. In your life, how do you respond when faith goes against logic? Have you ever had the experience of giving up to God something precious to you, something you considered a treasured gift from God?

10. How did Abraham earn the title "friend of God"? (Isaiah 41:8; James 2:21-23).

Perspectives on the Obedience Crisis

• If one dwells in Sodom, he ought not to be surprised that some of Sodom dwells in him.
• The entreaties of righteous men and women do make a difference in the course of history.
• God often allows tests in the lives of the faithful.

Abraham, Isaac, and Jacob in Canaan

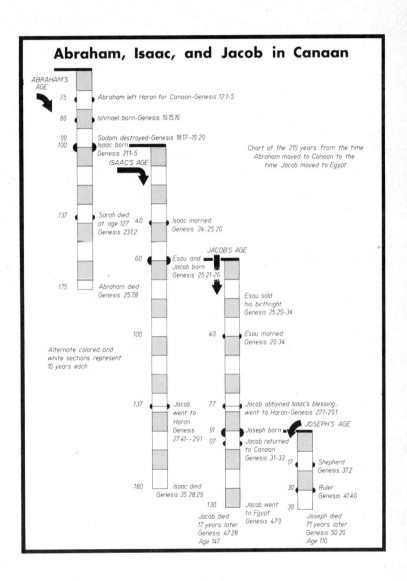

ABRAHAM'S AGE

75 — Abraham left Haran for Canaan-Genesis 12:1-5

86 — Ishmael born-Genesis 16:15,16

99 — Sodom destroyed-Genesis 18:17--19:29
100 — Isaac born
Genesis 21:1-5

ISAAC'S AGE

Chart of the 215 years from the time
Abraham moved to Canaan to the
time Jacob moved to Egypt

137 — Sarah died
at age 127
Genesis 23:1,2

40 — Isaac married
Genesis 24; 25:20

JACOB'S AGE

60 — Esau and
Jacob born
Genesis 25:21-26

175 — Abraham died
Genesis 25:7,8

Esau sold
his birthright
Genesis 25:29-34

100

40 — Esau married
Genesis 26:34

Alternate colored and
white sections represent
10 years each

137 — Jacob
went to
Haran
Genesis
27:41--29:1

77 — Jacob obtained Isaac's blessing,
went to Haran-Genesis 27:1-29:1

91 — Joseph born

JOSEPH'S AGE

97 — Jacob returned
to Canaan
Genesis 31-33

17 — Shepherd
Genesis 37:2

180 — Isaac died
Genesis 35:28,29

30 — Ruler
Genesis 41:46

39

130 — Jacob went
to Egypt
Genesis 47:9

Jacob died
17 years later
Genesis 47:28
Age 147

Joseph died
71 years later
Genesis 50:26
Age 110

8

Crisis
in Self-Interest
Genesis 23—28:9

A Princess Goes Home

Though she was ninety when she bore Isaac, Sarah lived long enough to see him grow to faithful manhood. She is the only woman in the whole of Scripture whose age is mentioned. She died at 127, thirty-seven years after the birth of that son who brought such laughter into her life (23:1).

We are told that Abraham came to Hebron to mourn and to weep for her. In all the vicissitudes of their life together, we are never before told in Scripture of Abraham's weeping. He had had many disappointments, separations, tragedies, and trials; but here, at Sarah's death, for the first time we see him in tears. His mind must have reviewed their years together—the departure from Ur; the sojourn in Haran; the famine in Canaan; the blunders in Egypt; the wanderings of nomads; the dug wells; the built altars; the growing prosperity; the swashbuckling rescue of Lot; his tithes to Melchizedek, king of Salem; his rejection of booty offered by the king of Sodom; the separation from Lot; the destruction of Sodom and Gomorrah; the compromising of Lot's character; the treaty with Abimelech; the waiting for a son; the fear for his life because of the beauty of Sarah; the attempt to bring about God's promises through Hagar; the contentiousness of his wives; the repeated covenant with God; the conversations with the angel of Jehovah; the visions; the prayers; the

66

laughter of Sarah as she cared for Isaac; the strange command that he offer his son as a sacrifice on Mount Moriah; the tents that had worn out in the dry wind of the Negev; the clear nights he had looked up to the stars and pondered the promise of God that his descendants would be without number; the providence and grace of God at every stage of his life—and Sarah, beautiful Sarah at his side through it all. She had been Sarai, the contentious one; she became Sarah, the princess.

Sarah, like Abraham, had grown in faith and trust in God as she had seen His promises fulfilled. "Through faith also Sarah herself received strength to conceive seed, and was delivered of a child when she was past age, because she judged him faithful who had promised" (Hebrews 11:11). Abraham and Sarah had experienced much together. They had failed at times, but the grace of God continually had been their salvation. Sarah had urged her husband to presumptuous action. She had brought dispute and ill feeling into his tent. She had laughed at the promise of God. But she had triumphed in faith, had seen the promise of God fulfilled in her old age, and had learned to walk with God through it all. It is no wonder that Abraham's heart was heavy when he laid her to rest.

Abraham and Sarah had spent their lives as nomads. Their possession of the land was still in promissory form. Sarah's death necessitated Abraham's first firm possession in the promised land. With stately Middle Eastern dignity, he approached the Hittites, the descendants of Heth, who dwelt near Hebron. His request was simple and straightforward. He did not wish to purchase a huge estate. All he wanted was a place to bury his beloved wife. He was still committed to the life of a pilgrim.

The owners of the land were quite deferential to him. They respected his sorrow and his position as the head of a wealthy clan. They offered him any sepulcher that he might desire. He requested that he might be permitted to buy a field and the cave of Machpelah from a man named Ephron. This man, in gracious fashion, urged Abraham to take the field and cave as a gift. Abraham insisted that he must buy them. The stately dialogue went back and forth with typical Middle Eastern diplomacy and tact, until Ephron, still insisting that Abraham take the land as a gift, noted that it was worth four hundred shekels of silver (23:15). In this roundabout way the price was set. Abraham did not haggle. He gave full price. Mamre had been a favorite place for Abraham and Sarah. It was there, in the cave of Machpelah, that the family sepulcher was established. Today, if one visits Hebron, he can enter a mosque that has been built over this cave that became the burial place not only of Sarah, but also of Abraham (25:9), Isaac, Rebekah, Leah (49:31), and Jacob (50:13). It is quite possible, were excavation allowed, that some remains of these worthies of old would be found.

A Bride for Isaac

Sarah's death and his own advanced age caused Abraham's mind to turn to the problem of finding a suitable wife for the son of the covenant, Isaac. Isaac's marriage was extremely important for the faithfulness of the descendants of the "line of promise." Abraham did not want his son to marry a Canaanite woman, a pagan who did not know God. With great solemnity, he commissioned his oldest and most trusted servant to return to Mesopotamia to find a wife for Isaac (24:1-9). To our way of thinking, it seems strange that Isaac himself did not make the journey. Though he lived in a time of arranged marriages, Abraham's servant also thought it strange that Isaac would not accompany him (24:5). Perhaps, the servant thought, he might not be able to find a suitable woman who would come such a great distance on faith. But Abraham was insistent that Isaac not accompany this expedition. Abraham relied on God to send His angel to direct his servant to a suitable wife for this son through whom so much of God's plan for mankind would be fulfilled (24:7). The servant, after solemnly swearing to fulfill Abraham's desires, set off to the east with a number of men and ten of Abraham's best camels.

The servant recognized Rebekah as God's choice for Isaac. The record of this is a tender and interesting story (24:10-67). It is clear that this trusted servant had been affected by his long comradeship with Abraham. His venture was bathed from beginning to end in prayer (24:12-14, 26, 27, 42-44, 48, 52). The Biblical account and the servant's speech are filled with references to the Lord's providence and participation in the events of life (24:21, 31, 35, 40, 50, 51, 56). There is also in the account an urgency, a sense of haste and glad expectation (24:15, 17, 20, 29, 33, 45, 46, 54-56).

One wonders what must have been in the mind of Isaac as he saw his father's oldest and most respected overseer preparing his camel caravan to depart toward Mesopotamia. He was approaching 40 and as yet had not married. His mother had recently died. His father, more than 137 years old now, was perhaps giving his son more and more responsibility. Isaac knew the prophecies concerning his father and the great nation that was to come from him. He knew that he was the child of promise. Was he getting a little impatient? Had he ever talked of marrying? What did he think of his father's idea of sending a servant to find a bride for him among their kindred back in Mesopotamia? What did he think of his father's insistence that he not accompany this expedition? Later, as the bridal expedition returned, we are told that Isaac was out in a field in the evening meditating (24:63). We can imagine that there was a lot of meditation and prayer in Isaac's mornings and evenings as he waited and wondered during the days of the caravan's absence. Doubtless his eyes went frequently toward the eastern horizon as he watched for that distinctive lumbering line of camels he and his father had so hopefully sent on their way. His mother had been a woman of exceeding beauty—so beautiful that Abraham had lived in constant fear that she would be stolen away from him, so beautiful that she had been coveted by influential men in both Egypt and Canaan. Would the woman who would return with his father's servant be anything like his mother? Would this old servant of his father see as he saw, understand what kind of wife would be best for him, and handle the matter with wisdom? Such a thought pattern would seem natural to us. But there was another thought pattern that may have overridden all these human concerns. Isaac had been placed on an altar at the command of God. He had heard his father say, when asked about a lamb for sacrifice, "The Lord will provide." Over and over he had heard his father speak of God's providence, of God's grace and lovingkindness. He had heard words of prayer and thanksgiving. Undoubtedly he had heard his father calling upon the name of the Lord on his son's behalf. He knew of the problems that impatience had brought in the matter of his half-brother Ishmael. He must certainly have believed, as his father did, that God would send His angel to guide this quest (24:7).

Isaac must certainly have looked on as his father's trusted servant chose from his father's animals the very best camels, as he wrapped and hid among the baggage some silver and gold jewelry and costly garments. Did he himself choose some of those gifts from among his father's treasures? As he held them up to the light and examined them for quality of workmanship, did he visualize the beautiful face and body that might soon display them?

We can only imagine these things, for the Biblical narrative ignores them completely. The focus of the Bible account is almost completely on the servant and on God. There is a sense of haste, as we have noted. The whole journey to Mesopotamia is summed up in one verse (24:10). This was a major trip, filled with dangers and long hours of swaying on the backs of camels, perhaps unexpected meetings and long conversations. Yet the Bible writer whisks us to Mesopotamia and to a well outside Haran.

We can picture the scene. The hand-dug well was merely an open hole in the ground, perhaps with a low wall of kiln-burned brick encircling it to keep children and small animals from falling in. The walls of the well were probably lined with brick to keep the well from caving in. In the wall around the well were deep grooves, evidence of the countless ropes that had been dragged against them as water had been drawn from the well for human refreshment and for herds and flocks of animals. Around the well were low watering troughs where sheep, goats, and camels came to sink their noses into cool, welcome refreshment. Wells were important centers of activity in ancient times, even as they remain today in the parched land of Mesopotamia. Each morning and evening, water was carried from the well to individual houses in the village. Young women in that day had no need to shape up before the television set each morning, for they were accustomed to aerobic water carrying. Today the women in that area wrap a small piece of cloth in a circle on their heads and carry there the clay water pots. When they return to their mud-brick houses, the water is poured into larger clay pots. The porosity of the pots allows water to seep through the sides, there to evaporate and thus cool the water within the pot.

Abraham's servant brought his camels to the well of Haran as the sun began to glow orange in the west. In Mesopotamia today that is a particularly welcome time of day. Midday is blisteringly hot during much of the year. But as the sun begins to set over the flat mud plains, there comes a refreshing coolness and an occasional breeze. The servant's camels knelt down, in that funny, awkward way that camels do. The servant prayed for God's leading. He knew, of course, that many of the young women of that town would come to draw water there at that time of day. They would undoubtedly gossip, banter, and laugh together as they pulled their vessels from the well on long ropes and began the walk back to their homes. It was not by accident that Abraham's servant stopped at that particular place at that particular time of day.

The servant had used intelligence and good judgment in his strategy, but he did not intend to rely on these for the choice of a bride for Isaac. He wanted that to be in the hands of God. He was much in prayer over the matter. He asked that God would show kindness to his master, Abraham, in showing the young woman who was God's choice. The servant asked God to identify her by her kindness and hospitality, her willingness to draw water both for him and for his camels. It was a big order, for a dry camel can drink up to twenty gallons of water. Multiply that by ten and you have a rather formidable project, not one to be undertaken casually. The signs that the servant asked for would indicate a young woman of hospitality, kindness, personal warmth, industry, and a giving spirit; but the servant's prayer indicated that he saw in them not so much a revelation of a young woman's character as a revelation of God's choice for Isaac (24:14).

The servant had no sooner finished his prayer than Rebekah came strolling out to the well, pitcher on her shoulder, for the evening water run. Little did she realize that there awaited her a meeting that would change her life. The servant noted her coming. She was attractive—that was a plus. She wore the costume of an unmarried woman—that was promising. She filled her water pot and hoisted it to her shoulder, the cool water dripping down the pot's side as she did so. The servant, little conscious of his dignity and eager to put her to the test, ran to her, requesting a drink. The work of water carrying is largely in the drawing of the water from the well and lifting the full water pot to the shoulder or head. Many women help one another lift a heavy pot for a friend. Once it is in place, however, one woman can walk easily with the heavy weight balanced above her.

The woman might, as the servant ran toward her, have been frightened to death. She might, as the servant asked her for a drink, have replied that he should seek his drink from someone who had not yet lifted her pot to her shoulder. She might have pointed out that she had no desire to walk back to her house with less than a full pot—he should get his drink from another. If any of these things went through her mind at all, we are not told. She simply stopped, lifted down her heavy water pot, and poured him out a drink.

The servant noted the encouraging fact that the attractive young woman had not shown fright when he came running toward her. She did not seem annoyed at his request and she responded promptly and courteously. He was watching carefully, listening closely. What would she say next? He must have smiled inwardly when she, noting his ten camels, volunteered to draw water for them as well. She returned to the well, then walked quickly back and forth from well to trough, pouring out the water for the thirsty dromedaries. The servant must have looked on in amazement and thanksgiving as he saw his prayer fulfilled before his eyes. She moved with authority, heaving up the heavy water-filled pot, hoisting it up, walking to the troughs, pouring the water out—all of this far above and beyond the demands of normal hospitality.

The first indications of God's desires in this matrimonial matter were clear, but the servant needed other signs of confirmation as well. It was important that he know of her people. Were they worshipers of God, or heathen like the Canaanites? After giving her gifts of a gold earring and gold bracelets, he asked about her family. His sense of God's providence was once again confirmed by her reply— she was a granddaughter of Abraham's brother.

There being no Holiday Inns in those days, it was customary for people on journeys to stay in private homes. When the servant asked if there was room for his company of people and his camels to stay at her home, Rebekah charmingly welcomed him. The servant heaved a sigh of relief and joy. God had truly answered his prayer. Rebekah ran back to her house to share the remarkable news with her mother and brother; and the servant, bemused by the fact that this lovely young woman was of Abraham's clan, lifted a prayer of thanks to God.

Meanwhile, back at Rebekah's house, words were flying. When her brother Laban saw the gold gifts and heard of her encounter with the stranger at the well, he rushed out to welcome the man and his party. Before long the camels were unloaded and provided for, the tired feet were washed, and food was placed before the visitors.

Abraham's servant, however, had only one thing on his mind. He would not eat until he had shared with his hosts the wonderful story of his master, his mission, and the answer to his prayer. Almost breathlessly he recounted the greatness and prosperity of his master, Abraham, the providence of God in the birth of Isaac, and Abraham's desires for his son of promise. He recounted the faith of Abraham and the wonderful way God had answered the prayer at the well. In particular, the servant thanked God for leading him to a woman who was a close relative of Abraham. Coming to the conclusion of his narrative, the servant made his request for Rebekah to become the wife of Isaac.

Bethuel, Rebekah's father, was the son of Nahor, Abraham's brother (22:20-23). Possibly he was very old and feeble at the time, or disabled by disease, for Rebekah's brother Laban and her mother were the ones most active in this matter. However, Laban and Bethuel both agreed that what had befallen was of the Lord, so their own thoughts on the matter seemed irrelevant. They agreed, saying, "Take her, and go, and let her be thy master's son's wife, as the Lord hath spoken" (24:51).

It was now confirmed. All the pieces fitted together. The servant gave thanks to God, gave gifts to Rebekah and her family, and ate and relaxed at last (24:52-54).

The servant arose and was ready to be off for home early the next morning. This man was old, but he was not one to dillydally in his assigned tasks. All of this seemed a bit hasty to Rebekah's mother and brother. They would have liked a few days to get used to the idea of her leaving. Abraham's servant, however, was insistent. In the end it was left up to Rebekah herself. She already had her bags packed and was ready to go (24:58).

It must certainly have taken great faith on her part for Rebekah to set out on this long journey, with a group of men she scarcely knew, to marry a man whom neither she nor her family had ever met. Yet she and her nurse and some maidservants joined the caravan with faith and anticipation (24:59-61).

Here Comes the Bride

The narrative climaxes as the caravan approaches Abraham's encampment. Isaac sees them coming and goes to meet them. Rebekah, her heart beating loudly, is straining her eyes for her first look at her prospective husband. Preserving the feminine mystique and doubtless arousing his curiosity to unbearable proportions, she demurely drops a veil over her face (24:62-65). Stedman, thinking of the stumbling first words of love, describes the meeting thus:

> This strong, manly man came up to her and said, "Hello."
> She said, "Hello."
> He said, "Are you Rebekah?"
> She said, "Yes," and dropped her eyes.
> Then he said, "I'm Isaac." (She knew it all the time.)
> He said, "You can call me Ike."
> She said, "Well, my friends call me 'Becky.'"
> And off they go hand in hand.[1]

---

1. Ray C. Stedman, *Discovery Paper*, No. 3673, © 1968. Used by permission of Discovery Publishing, Palo Alto, California.

Doubtless, in actual fact, the meeting began a bit more formally than that. But Stedman's dialogue catches the tone of their meeting. The servant couldn't wait to tell everyone how God had identified Rebekah, and how wonderful it was that she was of Abraham's clan and a worshiper of the true God. The wedding took place soon after, when Isaac was forty years old (25:20). They took up residence in the tent that had been Sarah's, and "he loved her" (24:66, 67). The closing statement of this dramatic narrative is rather an understatement—"and Isaac was comforted after his mother's death."

While Rebekah is certainly a central figure in all this, the story focuses most brightly on God and Abraham's unnamed servant. We are reminded that God was continuing to bless and care for Abraham and his seed. We hear expressed the simple, trusting prayers of the faithful servant as he continually called on the name of the God of Abraham, who had become his own God.

Abraham's Last Days and Death

In chapter 25 of Genesis, the spotlight swings back to Abraham, who lived for thirty-eight years after the death of his beloved Sarah. He married again and, wonder of wonders, was the father of six more children by Keturah. Remembering, perhaps, his difficulties with his first two sons, Abraham sent the children of his later years away from himself and Isaac, to the east. Finally, at the age of 175, the faithful patriarch was "gathered to his people" (25:7-11). The two sons who had been the subject of so much controversy, Isaac and Ishmael, buried him with honor and respect beside Sarah in the cave of Machpelah. Abraham had been generous with all his family, but Isaac was the recipient of God's special blessing (25:11) and the bulk of Abraham's possessions (25:5). He and Rebekah pitched their tent near the well of Lahairoi in the edge of the southern desert.

Like Father, Like Son

Isaac's life is not so fully narrated as the life of his father or the lives of his sons. We are given glimpses of Isaac's early life, as we have seen, and of his late life, as we shall see, but his middle years go largely unrecorded.

There are, however, a number of striking parallels between the lives of Abraham and his son Isaac. Both had to wait some time for the birth of their children. Rebekah did not give birth for twenty years after her marriage to Isaac. This was a period of prayer and supplication, which undoubtedly strengthened Isaac's awareness that his sons were a gift of God's grace (25:21). Isaac and Rebekah had to endure a famine, but God told them not to go into Egypt as Abraham had done (26:1-5). God also repeated the covenant promises to Isaac (26:2-5). Moving among strangers, Isaac tried to pass Rebekah off as his sister, even as his father had twice done with Sarah (26:6-11). Isaac, like his father, was blessed with material abundance (26:12-16), was troubled with envy from his neighbors, and endured disputes between his servants and their neighbors (26:15-23). He seems to have been a man of peace. When the herdsmen of Gerar kept appropriating his wells, he merely instructed his people to continue digging until there were enough wells for all (26:19-22). He also entered into an agreement with Abimelech, which was similar to the one Abraham had made with an earlier chief with the same name (26:26-33; 21:22-32). Perhaps Isaac's greatest similarity to his father, however, is recorded in 26:25: "And he builded an altar there [in Beersheba], and called upon the name of the Lord."

Maneuvering

In the latter part of chapter 25, the spotlight of Genesis swings away from Isaac and Rebekah to focus on their twin sons, Esau and Jacob.

Esau, the firstborn, was a gifted hunter who delighted his father with the food he put on the family table. Jacob, the homebody, was the apple of his mother's eye (25:28). Family favoritism frequently brings trouble in the home. So it was in the home of Isaac and Rebekah.

One day there came a notable confrontation between the homebody cook and the gadabout hunter. Jacob was at the cooking pot, stirring up a gastronomical delight of red lentils. Esau came in, all exhausted and famished from chasing after deer (25:29, 30).

Jacob was not so bighearted as his father and grandfather. He was not above using Esau's hunger for his own advantage. Now Esau came to the boiling caldron, took a whiff of the savory stuff, and like many an unsuccessful hunter since, exclaimed, "Boy, am I starved! Give me a bite of that red stuff there!" (25:30, LB).

This was the moment Jacob had been watching for. His elder brother seemed perfectly set up for his best curve ball. Jacob said, "All right, trade me your birthright for it!" (25:31, LB).

Esau answered recklessly: "When a man is dying of starvation, what good is his birthright?" (25:32, LB).

Then Jacob threw his fast ball, straight to the point: "Well then, vow to God that it is mine!" (25:33, LB).

Esau went for it. He vowed a vow as he passed his bowl, and struck out. He was out of his rightful place as chieftain of his clan and ruler over the family, out of his right to all the blessings that God had promised to Abraham and his line. Esau wolfed down the food, little realizing the price he had paid for his lunch. "So he ate and drank and went on about his business, indifferent to the loss of the rights he had thrown away" (25:34, LB).

While we can hardly approve of Jacob's treatment of his elder brother, we must come down strongly against Esau's indifference to the long-range values of life. Esau seems the perfect model of the person whose whole world is the sensual enjoyment of the present. Because the birthright was of little practical value at the moment, Esau frivolously threw it away. It doesn't seem at all inconsistent that such a one might be deemed unworthy to head the family God had chosen to be His special people and finally to bring blessing to the whole world. The writer of Hebrew calls Esau a profane person (Hebrews 12:16). He not only disregarded his own future welfare; he put no value on the promises of God.

Esau's marriages too were indicative of his short-sighted nature. At the age of forty, he married two heathen Hittites, who surely would not help to keep the family faithful to God. These marriages were a sore trial to his parents (26:34, 35).

Masquerading

In the earlier narrative, we have discovered Rebekah to be industrious, good-natured, adventurous, trusting, demure, and beautiful. But one less-attractive trait finally showed itself. She was a scheming woman. Determined that her favorite son, Jacob, should supplant her elder son, she encouraged him to deceive his ailing and aging father, Isaac, in order to receive a blessing that was not rightfully his (27:1-29). It is not surprising that Jacob grew up more than a little sneaky.

Even before the boys were born, God had said the elder would serve the younger (25:23). But Rebekah was not content to wait for God to bring this about in His own way and His own time. Seeing an opportunity, she decided to give things a little human push, even if it disregarded truth and honesty. She and Jacob acted out a lie to fool Isaac. Taking advantage of Isaac's bad sight, they tricked him and lied to him (27:6-29).

Rebekah knew that Isaac intended to confer his blessing on Esau when the young man came back from a deer-hunting expedition with venison for his father. While he was gone, Rebekah and Jacob killed some goats and prepared meat to deceive the nearly blind Isaac. Jacob was wary of his mother's plan, however. He knew his father would recognize the difference between the two boys, for Esau was rough and hairy while Jacob was smooth skinned (27:11). But Rebekah covered Jacob's arms and neck with the hairy skin of young goats (27:16). She also brought some of Esau's clothes for Jacob to put on so he would smell like Esau (27:15, 26, 27).

Jacob took the food to his father, identified himself as Esau, and lied about the source of food. By means of his body odor and his covered hands and neck, he overcame Isaac's doubts as to the voice he heard (27:18-23). Isaac, thus deceived, pronounced the blessing:

> Therefore God give thee of the dew of heaven, and the fatness of the earth, and plenty of corn and wine: let people serve thee, and nations bow down to thee: be lord over thy brethren, and let thy mother's sons bow down to thee: cursed be every one that curseth thee, and blessed be he that blesseth thee.
>
> —Genesis 27:27-29

By this ruse, Jacob received the blessing that was intended for his older brother.

To us it may seem that too much importance was attached to the blessing of an old man. However, the patriarchs of God's people were not ordinary old men. God used them as prophets to express His will. Abraham is called a prophet (20:7). This blessing given by Isaac turned out to be a true prophecy. See also Jacob's prophetic blessing of his sons at a later time (Genesis 49). The blessing did not compel God to bring about what it asked, but God inspired the prophet to foretell what God knew would happen.

When Esau returned, he cooked his venison and took it to his father, only to find that the blessing had already been given. Isaac was deeply disturbed. Esau was heartbroken. He wept and cried out for a blessing from his father. When he realized that his brother had displaced him with trickery, he wailed, "Is not he rightly named Jacob? for he hath supplanted me these two times: he took away my birthright; and, behold, now he hath taken away my blessing" (27:36). The name *Jacob* means one who catches another's heel or trips him (25:24-26). Since a runner may trip another in order to take his place or supplant him, the name means also a supplanter. Esau said Jacob had lived up to it twice.

Esau entreated his father for a blessing, but Isaac could not give to him what already had been given to Jacob. Finally Isaac said to Esau, "Behold, thy dwelling shall be the fatness of the earth, and of the dew of heaven from above; and by thy sword shalt thou live, and shalt serve thy brother: and it shall come to pass when thou shalt have the dominion, that thou shalt break his yoke from off thy neck" (27:39, 40). Esau, full of bitterness and hate, determined to kill his crafty brother as soon as their aged father was gone from the scene (27:41).

So Jacob's ruse was successful. He and his mother had their way, but they were to pay a high price for taking things into their own hands. Had they been content to wait on God to bring about His promise in His own good time, things undoubtedly would have worked out better. As it was, a terrible rift was created in the family (27:41-45).

Because of Esau's vow to kill him, Jacob had to flee from his home. Rebekah put a good face on it all to Isaac, saying that Jacob was going to the land of her family to find a wife (27:46). The old man sent Jacob on his way with a blessing (28:1-5), but the parting was clouded by the deception that had gone before.

Rebekah sent her son out to receive his own share of trickery at the hands of others (29:21-30). So far as we know, the mother never saw her favorite son again. She got her way in the matter of the blessing, but it was costly.

Ironically, it seems that Jacob's flight was not really necessary. Esau proposed to postpone his vengeance till Isaac died (27:41). Probably he thought that would be soon, as Isaac himself did (27:4). But as a matter of fact, Isaac was still living when Jacob came back and the brothers were reconciled after twenty years (35:27-29).

Abraham had sent a servant to Mesopotamia to bring a wife suitable for his son, Isaac. God had managed that simply, beautifully, and effectively. Rebekah and Isaac were now sending their son on a similar journey on his own behalf (28:1-5). This journey set in motion by deception would continue in bitterness. Jacob had some lessons to learn during the following twenty years of separation from his family.

While Esau attempted to ingratiate himself with his parents by further marriages (28:6-9), Jacob journeyed toward Padan-aram.

78

How would God use this selfish, striving man? We shall see a gradual hammering of his willful character. If ever anyone's life illustrated the grace, the unmerited favor, of God, Jacob's did.

This chapter began with prayer, trust in God, and happiness in God's loving providence. It ended with duplicity, deceit, hatred, fear, and separation. What a contrast between Abraham's servant's journey to Mesopotamia and the fearful flight of Jacob to that same country! There is within human nature a grasping spirit, a competitiveness, a desire to manipulate things to personal advantage. This spirit, when allowed to flourish, leads to lying, deceit, alienation, discord, and separation. The one who trusts in God, by contrast, is continually surprised by joy and happiness.

What we give, we get. Little did Jacob know, at his moment of seeming victory, that he was soon to be a victim of the deceptions of others.

For Reflection

1. What real estate did Abraham buy in Canaan? What continuing significance did this place have?

2. What kind of person was sent to find a wife for Isaac? What evidences of faith do we find in his words and actions?

3. How did the messenger choose the right person to be Isaac's wife?

4. What kind of person did Rebekah seem to be when she was singled out to be Isaac's wife? What kind of person did she seem to be later, in securing Isaac's blessing for Jacob?

5. What similarities are seen between Abraham's life and that of Isaac? What differences?

6. How were Jacob and Esau different? What favoritism appeared in the family? (25:27, 28).

7. What action of Esau particularly grieved his parents? (26:34, 35). How did he try later to gain their favor? (28:8, 9).

8. How did Jacob cheat Esau out of his birthright? (25:29-34). How was each of them at fault in this matter?

9. By duplicity Rebekah and Jacob brought about what God had predicted for her two sons (25:23). Do you think God was pleased with what they did?

10. In the events recorded in Genesis 27, whom do you feel most sorry for—Isaac, Rebekah, Jacob, or Esau?

Perspectives on the Self-Interest Crisis

- "Trust in the Lord with all your heart, and do not rely on your own insight" (Proverbs 3:5, RSV).
- Esau disregarded his birthright because it had no immediate value to him. Jacob valued it so highly that he went to unscrupulous lengths to obtain it. Both were wrong. Neither one truly trusted in God.
- "See to it . . . that no one be immoral or irreligious like Esau, who sold his birthright for a single meal. For you know that afterward, when he desired to inherit the blessing, he was rejected, for he found no chance to repent, though he sought it with tears" (Hebrews 12:15-17, RSV).
- God promised preeminence to Jacob, but Jacob was not willing to rely on God to fulfill His word. He gave things a nudge, and suffered estrangement and exile as a result of his duplicity.
- "Don't be selfish; don't live to make a good impression on others. Be humble, thinking of others as better than yourself. Don't just think about your own affairs, but be interested in others, too, and in what they are doing" (Philippians 2:3, 4, LB).

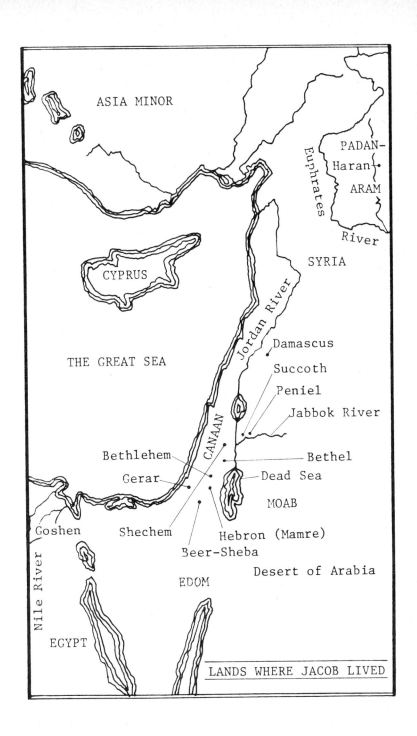

ASIA MINOR

PADAN-
Haran
ARAM

Euphrates
River

SYRIA

CYPRUS

Jordan River

THE GREAT SEA

Damascus
Succoth
Peniel
Jabbok River

CANAAN

Bethlehem
Gerar

Bethel
Dead Sea

MOAB

Goshen

Shechem
Hebron (Mamre)
Beer-Sheba

Desert of Arabia

Nile River

EDOM

EGYPT

LANDS WHERE JACOB LIVED

9

Crisis
in Relationship
Genesis 28:10—32:32

As he journeyed east toward Haran, Jacob may have thought of his grandfather Abraham's westward journey across the same terrain. Abraham's journey had been set in motion by faith. Jacob's had been set in motion by fear.

The Vision

One night while the tired traveler slept with his head on a stone for a pillow, Jacob dreamed. He saw a great ladder reaching from the earth to Heaven. Angels were ascending and descending, and God himself stood above it (28:10-13). In this dramatic vision, God repeated His covenant promise to this privileged descendant of Abraham and Isaac (28:13-15).

This blessing involved no trickery. And it was certainly not because Jacob had shown great goodness. He was selfish and crooked, but God had great purposes for this fleeing son of Isaac.

This was one of two great divine confrontations for Jacob. Here he was confronted with the majesty of God and the glories of God's plan for him and his posterity. This confrontation impressed Jacob deeply (28:16-19). The second would come twenty years later when Jacob was journeying west along the same road that now took him east (32:24-32). Both encounters came at moments of fear and uncertainty. While God spoke of great things for Jacob's posterity,

Jacob seems to have been most impressed by those promises involving his personal safety and prosperity (28:15, 20-22). If God would protect and provide for him, Jacob vowed, then he would be faithful in remembrance and in offerings. It may be noted that he did not vow to be kind and generous.

Love

Finally Jacob arrived at Haran, the chief town of the district of Padan-aram. Like Abraham's servant who had found Rebekah, Jacob now used a well as a means of meeting the people of the area (29:1-20). There his eyes first fell on Rachel, a young lady so lovely that a month later Jacob volunteered to work seven years for her hand in marriage (29:17, 18). Jacob was hopelessly in love; in fact, the seven years he worked for Laban, her father, "seemed unto him but a few days, for the love he had to her" (29:20).

Laban and his nephew, Jacob, were "birds of a feather." They were both "smart operators," bargainers, inveterate con men. When the time at last came for Jacob's marriage according to the long-standing bargain, the wily Laban switched brides on his unsuspecting son-in-law (29:21-26). It was, he said, not fitting that the younger should be married before the older. Seven years, and he had not gotten around to explaining this little detail to Jacob!

Laban was ready with another bargain. He had successfully gotten rid of his homely daughter (29:17), but Jacob was still a good match for Rachel as well. Bargaining shrewdly, he extracted another seven years of labor from the love-struck suitor. Perhaps he even felt rather magnanimous in granting Rachel on a deferred payment plan. After only seven days of marriage to Leah, Jacob could have Rachel and could work off her payment later (29:27-30).

Rivalry

Jacob's family life was turbulent, to say the least. His father-in-law, so he thought, took advantage of him continually. He responded by taking advantage of his father-in-law. There was constant suspicion, bickering, and dissension. Rachel was Jacob's favorite wife, but Leah was the one who bore him children. The two wives were bitter rivals (29:31—30:21).

When Rachel saw that Leah was having all the babies, she was so jealous that she urged Jacob to have children by her servant. (Shades of Hagar!) Leah, not to be outdone, urged Jacob to have children by *her* servant girl. Leah's team pulled ahead in the contest. For a long time the score was nine children for Leah's team (six sons and one daughter for Leah, two sons for her servant), and two for Rachel's team (two sons for Rachel's servant). Rachel wasn't even in the contest, until she finally bore Joseph (30:22-24).

While the ladies were trying to gain supremacy in their sphere, Laban and Jacob had their own rivalry going. At the end of fourteen years both his wives were paid for, and Jacob decided to return to the land of his fathers. But Laban saw that it was not in his interest to lose this major asset. He had observed that God prospered his son-in-law. The two men bargained. Finally, Jacob agreed to continue his labor for Laban, this time working not for wives but for wool (30:25-36).

Jacob, the conniver, was in his element. In whatever way possible, he saw to it that his flock grew at the expense of Laban's (30:37-43). His stratagems were effective, or else the gracious hand of God poured out prosperity to this descendant of Abraham despite his machinations. Whatever the reason, his flocks and possessions increased remarkably.

Jealousy

With prosperity came jealousy. Wealth gained at the expense of others has its own hazards. Laban's sons howled and Laban scowled (31:1, 2). The sons claimed that Jacob had taken what was rightfully theirs. It was an appropriate time for Jacob to take his winnings and run. This is exactly what he decided to do. Yet God was still with Jacob. It was God who cast the deciding vote for Jacob's return to the land of his fathers (31:3). Jacob consulted with his wives, and they were of the same mind (31:4-16).

Departure

Now all that remained was the getaway. The exit was planned in typical Jacob fashion—nothing open and straightforward if there is a covert and devious way to be found.

Jacob's bags were packed. He was ready to go. The occasion for a secret departure came when Laban went off to a sheepshearing. Without so much as a word of farewell to the man for whom he had worked for twenty years and whose daughters he had married, Jacob and his family vamoosed, moving their flocks ahead of them as fast as they could (31:17-21).

Meanwhile, back at the shearing, Laban got wind of what was afoot. Jacob had three days head start on him, but the trail was still warm. Laban mounted up with his men and galloped after Jacob (31:22, 23). Having family and flocks, Jacob moved slowly. It took only a week for Laban to catch him.

Verbal Shoot-out

What Laban intended to do about Jacob's defection we do not know. But one night, while on the trail of his fleeing son-in-law, Laban had a dream in which God told him, "Watch out what you say to Jacob. Don't give him your blessing and don't curse him" (31:24, LB). That didn't leave many options.

Laban caught up with Jacob and proceeded to give him a first class tongue-lashing. "What do you mean by sneaking off like this? . . . Why didn't you give me a chance to have a farewell party? . . . Why didn't you let me kiss my grandchildren and tell them good-bye?" (31:26-28, LB).

Laban knew that Jacob had his own answer for all this. He had never treated Jacob very well and he knew it. As Jacob was getting his own tongue loaded up for a sharp reply, Laban, ever the shrewd strategist, charged Jacob with the theft of the family idols. Rachel, in fact, had taken them without Jacob's knowledge (31:19).

Jacob raged in righteous indignation. "I sneaked away because I was afraid," Jacob asserted. "I said to myself, 'He'll take his daughters from me by force'" (31:31, LB). As to the family idols, Jacob denied the charge of theft and challenged Laban to put up or shut up (31:32).

While Laban searched in vain for evidence, Jacob stoked his rage. (Rachel had hidden the idols in her camel saddle and she sat upon it during the entire search.) When Laban failed to produce proof positive of his charge, Jacob, now sure of his ground, let loose his strongest verbal barrage. All the hot anger that had built in him for the past twenty years came exploding out (31:36-42).

Having unloaded their vituperation, the two men at last came to the point where they began to listen to one another. Laban proposed that they quit railing and begin to think of the kinship that bound them together in love for the same women and children, if not for one another (31:43, 44). They entered into a peace pact, Laban committing the loving care of his daughters to Jacob and to God. They solemnized their nonaggression pact by setting up a symbolic heap of stones, agreeing not to cross, with hostile intent, the line marked by the stones (31:45-52). The pact was sealed with oaths, sacrifices, and feasting (31:53, 54).

The heap of stones became known as "Mizpah" or "Watchtower." It was to be a witness to them of their solemn compact. But the real witness was God. Laban said it well when he said, "May the Lord see to it that we keep this bargain when we are out of each other's sight" (31:49, LB).

At long last, the contention settled, Laban gave his daughters and grandchildren their farewell kiss (31:55). It is not mentioned that he kissed Jacob.

Fear

Jacob no longer had reason to fear the relative behind him, but the relative in front of him was another matter. What would be the attitude of his brother, Esau? Though two decades had passed, Jacob was afraid of this brother who had vowed to kill him. He sent a conciliatory message, saying that he was coming with a great company and asking that he might find favor in Esau's sight (32:1-5).

When the messengers returned with the news that Esau was on the way to meet him with four hundred men, Jacob trembled in his sandals. He carefully divided his party into two groups so that one might escape if Esau attacked (32:6-8). He sent a great many of his animals ahead of the main party as gifts (32:13-20). Then, under cover of night, he separated a third group (his wives, concubines, and eleven children) and saw it safely across the Jabbok River. Apparently he then returned to supervise the movement of the rest of the caravan as it crossed the river (32:22, 23).

Dependence

Fear motivated these precautions, even though God had promised to be with Jacob (31:3) and Jacob was aware of God's angels (32:1). He continued his human stratagems, but for the first time there seems to appear in Jacob's life some evidence of surrender to God. For the first time we hear him acknowledging sin and unworthiness and recognizing God's help (32:9-12).

This moment of crisis, when he stood in mortal fear for his life and the lives of those he loved, was a turning point in Jacob's life. He prayed, "O God of Abraham my grandfather, and of my father Isaac. . . . I am not worthy of the least of all your loving kindnesses shown me again and again just as you promised me. . . . O Lord, please deliver me." (32:9-11, LB).

Contrition and dependence on God were conquering self-reliance. Jacob was at last beginning to get it all together.

Confrontation

Family and caravan had gone across the river, and Jacob was left alone. That night a strange event occurred that would mark the transformation that was taking place in Jacob's life. He wrestled with an angel (32:24-32).

Twenty years earlier Jacob had received a spectacular vision and a message from God as he was leaving his homeland (28:10-22). Now he was returning to that land, and again God communicated with him in an unusual way.

Jacob's adversary appeared as a man (32:24), but Hosea (12:4) calls him an angel. Jacob himself made no distinction between God's messenger and God himself, saying, "I have seen God face to face" (32:30). While the encounter was certainly symbolic of what was taking place in Jacob's life, it was no less real and physical.

The combat raged throughout the night. As the dawn approached, Jacob was still holding his own. Then the angel touched Jacob's hip and knocked it out of joint at the socket. Still Jacob wouldn't give up. As the angel struggled, Jacob hung on for dear life, demanding a blessing.

Jacob's whole life had been one of struggling for blessing. He had connived for his birthright and lied for his father's blessing. Now he was desperate in his fear of Esau. He realized that the struggle with the angel might hold the key to the struggle with his brother. If ever he needed the blessing of God, it was at this moment.

The angel asked Jacob his name. "Jacob," was the reply. That was both a statement of fact and a confession. The name meant "heel catcher" or "supplanter." It had been given him because of the unusual manner of his birth (25:26), but it proved to be appropriate to his nature. His grasping ways had tripped up his brother, Esau, and caused contention with his father-in-law, Laban.

From now on, the angel indicated, Jacob would be called Israel, meaning "prince of God," "God's fighter," or "one who struggles with God." This new name would fit him, the angel said, "for as a prince hast thou power with God and with men, and hast prevailed" (32:28). Jacob proved to be a prince, not in his own strength but in his weakness. He prevailed when his own strength was exhausted and he could do nothing but cling to God's messenger and beg for a blessing.

· The newly named Israel sought the name of his wrestling opponent, but he was not told. The messenger's name was not important. He represented God, and that *was* important (32:29, 30).

Jacob limped away that morning with a dislocated hip. At every step he was reminded of his encounter with God. He had learned some painful lessons before, and this one also was painful. But now he not only had a new name; he had a new spirit.

He knew that his power was of God. He was not perfect from that day on, but he was God's man more completely than ever before. More than a mere wrestling match, Jacob's encounter was a spiritual transformation. He was prepared more fully than ever to accept God's provisions for his life.

Jacob's life was filled with troubled relationships. Rivalry, contention, deceit, trickery, conniving, recrimination, and ill will seemed to follow him everywhere he went. He was not at peace with man because he was not at peace with God. He was not living up to his high calling. How often this is true also of us who are Christians! It is in relationships that our faith must be lived out. Jacob lived with suspicion and fear because he had not learned to trust God for his welfare and because he had not learned the principle of loving others as himself.

For Reflection

1. As Jacob was running away from his brother's anger, how did a message from God come to him? What was the message? How did Jacob respond? Do you think this response showed maturity or immaturity? (28:10-22).

2. Describe three contracts Laban made with Jacob: one a month after Jacob arrived in Haran, one seven years later, and one after seven more years (29:15-30; 30:25-36). How did Jacob try to gain some advantage over Laban in building his flock? (30:37-43). How did Laban try to gain the advantage? (31:7).

3. Why did Jacob leave Haran? Why did he do it secretly? Why did Laban follow? What do you think Laban would have done if God had not warned him? What complaints did Laban make against Jacob? What complaints did Jacob make against Laban? How did these two settle their quarrel? (31:1-55).

4. What flaws do you see in the character of Laban? Of Jacob? Of Leah? Of Rachel? Which of the four would you least like to have as a business partner? (Chapters 29—31).

5. Why do you suppose God chose such a faulty character as Jacob to be the father of His chosen people?

6. Why was Jacob afraid as he went to meet his brother? How did he try to win his brother's favor?

7. Describe Jacob's contest with an angel. What do you think it meant? Why was a new name given to Jacob? What evidence do you see of spiritual growth in Jacob?

8. Why is it so easy for people to get caught up in avarice and rivalry?

9. How were God's grace and patience evidenced in His dealings with Jacob? How are they evidenced in His dealings with you?

10. What lessons for life do you see from the events of this lesson?

Perspectives on the Relationship Crisis

- Confrontation with God can be personally painful and humbling.
- Fear forced Jacob to his knees in prayer. Would that we prayed as earnestly when things are going well as we do when we find ourselves in personal danger.
- "Humble yourselves in the sight of the Lord, and he shall lift you up" (James 4:10).
- Like Jacob, those who resist God will find their lives out of joint.

10

Crisis
in Family
Genesis 33—37

More than Jacob's name was changed by his night of wrestling with the angel of God (32:24-32). He now approached Esau with a more humble spirit than he had when he fled from his wronged, hate-filled brother twenty years earlier. But what would Esau's attitude now be?

The moment of truth approached. "And Jacob lifted up his eyes, and looked, and, behold, Esau came, and with him four hundred men" (33:1). It was a confrontation filled with uncertainty and high drama. Would it be slaughter and death, or would it be love and brotherhood? Jacob did not know. But he did not turn and run.

Reconciliation

We can imagine the relief and the tears of joy that welled up in Jacob when that swarthy brother of his, whom he had tricked and cheated, "ran to meet him, and embraced him, and fell on his neck, and kissed him" (33:4). Time and the Spirit of God had done their work on Esau also. Rather than in bloody confrontation, these brothers met in happy reunion (33:2-4).

Then followed family introductions (33:5-7). Jacob offered Esau generous gifts, which he at first refused. God had blessed them both with prosperity. Jacob insisted, however, and Esau eventually accepted Jacob's peace offering (33:8-11). After some debate over whether they would proceed together or separately, the two brothers parted on friendly terms (33:12-17). Esau went back to his home in Seir, on the east side of the Dead Sea (33:16). Jacob proceeded by easy stages, stopping for a time at Succoch and then going on to pitch his camp near Shalem (33:17, 18).

Revenge

It is almost an axiom of life that children imitate their parents. Jacob's children had too few good examples to follow. They had witnessed deceit and self-service in their father, their mothers, and their uncle, and they had not come through unscathed. The Bible says, "For whatsoever a man soweth, that shall he also reap" (Galatians 6:7). Jacob himself had mellowed and matured in the Lord, but the time for the harvest of deceit was soon to come in his sons.

Jacob had eleven sons and one daughter, Dinah. She was seduced by Shechem, a Hivite, a prince of the area where Jacob had taken up residence. She was young by our standards, perhaps between thirteen and fifteen. But she was of marriageable age, and Shechem wanted her for his wife. Shechem's father, Hamor, went to negotiate the marriage with Jacob, though she was already in Shechem's house (34:26). But when Dinah's brothers learned what had happened to their sister, they were bent on revenge, not marriage (34:1-7).

Hamor, with oriental courtesy, proposed that Jacob's family intermarry with the people of the community. He offered a generous dowry for Dinah (34:8-12).

All of this stuck in the throats of Dinah's outraged brothers. They quite rightly refused to condone this crime against Israel and against God. But they chose wrongly to repay sin with treachery.

Simeon and Levi took the initiative in avenging the wrong done to their sister. On the surface, they seemed to agree to intermarriage with the Hivites. One problem, however, hindered it. The people of Abraham were circumcised. If Shechem and his clan would submit to this operation, Dinah's brothers assured Hamor, then all would be fine. The Hivites acquiesced, and while they were still sore from the operation, Simeon and Levi slaughtered all the men of the town. Apparently the rest of Jacob's sons joined these two and their servants in plundering Shalem, the city of the Hivites (34:13-29).

"Vengeance is sweet" is a common proverb. But vengeance has a way of begetting vengeance. Fear came in the wake of the bloody revenge taken by Jacob's sons. "Now you have done it," Jacob lamented. "You have made my name to stink in this land. Now they will join together to destroy us all" (34:30). Jacob saw the logical outcome of the brutality and savage plundering. The boys who had taken things into their own hands, however, were not sorry in the least. "Should we let him get away with treating our sister like a prostitute?" they said (34:31). Jacob, for all his love for his daughter, could not condone their savagery (49:5-7).

Return

In the midst of the uncertainty and fear created by the slaughter of the Hivites at Shalem, God commanded Jacob to return to Bethel, the place where he had met God and received the promise about thirty years before (35:1). Jacob then ordered that all the people of his household wash and put on clean clothes as a sign of the renewal symbolized by this return to the "house of God." The camp was also thoroughly purged of idols before Jacob's household set out through hostile territory to the place of promise (35:2-5). After building an altar at Bethel, Jacob once again received the Abrahamic promise (35:6-15).

The high religious moments, however, were not untouched by personal tragedy. Deborah, the nurse who had accompanied Rebekah when she left Haran to come to Isaac, died at Bethel (35:8). It is interesting that Deborah's death is noted in Scripture, though Rebekah's is not. We know that Rebekah was buried in the cave of Machpelah (49:31), but we are not told of her death. We also are not told when Deborah joined herself to Jacob's clan. Doubtless, however, Rachel missed this old family servant as her pregnancy drew to a close not long thereafter.

Rachel, Jacob's most beloved wife, had a very difficult delivery. Before she died, she knew that she had given birth to a son. As her life slipped from her, she named the boy Benoni, "son of my pain," or "of my sorrow." Jacob saw this child of his old age and of his most beloved wife in a different light. He called the boy Benjamin, "son of the right hand." Some students interpret this as "son of good fortune" (35:16-21).

As he buried his lovely Rachel near Bethlehem, Jacob must have remembered how he had first fallen in love with her at the well of Haran and how much she had desired such a son as the one he now held in his arms. She was buried near Bethlehem, not taken to the cave of Machpelah, the family burying place. This suggests that perhaps Jacob was not yet reconciled with his father, whom he had deceived just before he fled to Haran.

Perhaps we may read a few things between the lines here. Could it be that Rachel's death turned Jacob's mind to his father and to the bridging of the rift that was still between them? Would not he have wanted Isaac to meet Rachel, this beautiful wife of his whom he had met in circumstances so similar to those in which his mother had been found? Would not he have wanted the blessing of Isaac on his children? Would not he have wanted Rachel to be buried in the cave of Machpelah with his mother and his grandmother? Perhaps Jacob had been waiting for a propitious time to return to his father. Perhaps Rachel's unexpected death moved him to put it off no longer. At any rate, it was not long after her death that Jacob returned to Hebron, to that special oak at Mamre, to visit his aged father, Isaac (35:27). Isaac and Jacob must have had a great deal to talk about. Jacob was now a changed man, having purged his house of idols and his heart of self-worship. Not very many years later, Isaac died at the ripe old age of 180. It would have pleased him, surely, to see his two sons, Jacob and Esau, together again as they carried his body to the cave of Machpelah (35:29).

Partiality and Cruelty

Selfishness and deceit plagued the way of the youthful Jacob, as we have seen. These twin evils likewise stalked his old age, not so much in himself as in his sons. Reuben, his eldest son, became sexually involved with Rachel's handmaid, Bilhah, who was also Jacob's concubine (35:22). Jacob remembered that to his dying day (49:3, 4).

A family crisis of monumental proportions came when Joseph, Rachel's first son, was seventeen. This boy was Jacob's favorite, being a "son of his old age" and a son of his favorite wife. The more Jacob loved and favored Joseph, the more his other sons resented and hated him (37:3, 4).

Joseph got into hot water with his brothers by reporting to their father some of their mischief (37:2). Then too, he wore a special coat that had been given him by his father. So bitter did their jealousy become that Joseph's brothers could scarcely say a civil word to him.

The situation was aggravated as well by Joseph's dreams. Either innocently or with undue pride, Joseph told his hate-filled brothers of his nocturnal visions. In one dream Joseph and his brothers were binding grain in the fields. Suddenly the sheaves stood upright, and the sheaves of his brothers bowed down to his. Even if Joseph was cocky and arrogant in telling this, that hardly excuses his brothers for their reaction to a dream suggesting that Joseph would someday rule over them. "And they hated him yet the more for his dreams, and for his words"(37:5-8).

Perhaps the other sons were a little uncertain about their own place as heirs of Jacob. They knew their own father had not been the first son, yet he had received the birthright and blessing. They knew too that Joseph was the first son of Jacob's most loved wife. Would Jacob pass over the ten sons born to Leah and two servant girls in order to place Joseph at the head of the clan?

Favorite though Joseph was, his dreams did not set well with Jacob either. When Joseph recounted a dream that implied that not only his brothers but also his father would bow down to him, his father rebuked him. Probably this rebuke pleased his brothers, but still their envy and hatred increased. Later Jacob would have cause to remember these events which he now stored away in his heart (37:9-11).

Hatred, if harbored, hatches horrors. The day of crisis came when Joseph was sent by his father to see how his brothers were keeping the family flocks many miles from home (37:12-17).

As soon as the brothers saw that familiar bright-colored coat approaching, they conspired to deprive Joseph of his civil rights—by killing him. Their first plan was to murder their young brother, throw his body into some handy cistern or pit, and then put out the cover story that he had been killed by wild animals. That would fell the dreamer and foil the prophetic events his dreams seemed to portend (37:18-20).

Joseph, fortunately, had a secret ally among the conspirators. It was Reuben, the eldest, the one charged by custom with responsibility for looking out for younger brothers—and the one who would be superseded if Joseph's dreams came true.

Taking a bold stand against fratricide, Reuben suggested a slight change in plan. Rather than staining their hands with their brother's blood as had Cain, why not let nature do him in? Why not throw him into a deep pit from which he could not escape? He would die of thirst soon enough (37:21-24).

The next step in Reuben's plan was to slip back and pull his brother to safety. This intention was thwarted by a new factor, a passing camel caravan on its way to Egypt with spices. The spices were possibly intended for the elaborate funeral customs so common in the land of the Pharaohs.

Perhaps Judah, along with Reuben, was not pleased with the prospect of being directly responsible for the death of a brother. Or perhaps he thought there was no point in murder, when the same end could be accomplished without bloodshed and with a little profit from the deal (37:26-28).

Reuben was not there when Joseph was shanghaied to Egypt. When he returned to the pit to pull the properly humbled Joseph out, he found that it was empty. Though Reuben was remorseful and deeply worried about his brother, we are not told that he tried to rescue him (37:29, 30). Along with the others, he joined in the cover-up.

The conspirators dipped Joseph's coat in goat blood. What had been a coat of many colors now bore a scarlet stain. Jacob, as they knew he would, accepted their story that Joseph had been killed by wild animals. Jacob plunged into abject grief, while the deceitful sons joined with the rest of the family in trying to comfort their grieving father. It is not surprising that they were not very good at it (37:31-35).

Meanwhile, in Egypt, Joseph was sold to the captain of Pharaoh's guard.

Many of the crises we have studied in Genesis have been family crises—Cain and Abel, Abraham and Lot, Isaac and Ishmael, Jacob and Esau, Sarah and Hagar, Rachel and Leah. But chapters 33-37 seem particularly to focus on problems between family members. Here we see of the reconciliation of two brothers after the passage of many years of fear and bitterness. We observe the worthy concern of brothers for the welfare of their sister, but we see it corrupted into murder and pillage. We read of the reconciliation of an alienated son to his father just before the aged man's death. Finally, we see the dividing sword of favoritism and jealousy severing a family.

It is in the family that many of life's greatest battles are won or lost. In the decisions made by parents, one finds the key to much that unfolds in national life. Evil is passed on from generation to generation, even as righteousness bears good fruit in succeeding generations. There is probably no area of modern life that is more in need of God's redemption than the modern family. Children pick up predominant characteristics from their parents. Jacob, in later life, wrestled with the angel and came to learn dependence on God. By that time, however, his sons were already well formed. During their most formative years, the father they saw was the opportunist and the contender. It is no wonder that they became a grief to him and a reproach to God. They too had some lessons to learn. They would, before long, be humbled and their descendants would eventually be enslaved. Finally, God would come to their rescue and, in the wilderness of Sinai, educate them once again to the ways of faith.

History concentrates on major political movements and their outcomes. It focuses on wars, social upheaval, revolution, and scientific advances. Yet one wonders how history might have been different had Hitler's home or Marx's home been different. The family remains the most important teaching institution in the world. It is there that the individuals who shape history are formed, either for good or for evil.

For Reflection

1. Why was Jacob fearful as he neared his homeland? What was his strategy in approaching Esau? (32:3—33:11). Do you think that strategy was necessary?

2. What brought enmity between Jacob's family and their neighbors at Shalem? (34:1-31). What do the actions of Simeon and Levi and the other brothers reveal about their character? How did Jacob react to their conduct? (34:30, 31).

3. One writer notes that at Haran Jacob was redirected by God (31:1-16), at Peniel he was broken and restored by God (32:22-32), and at Bethel he was reassured by God (35:1-15). What similar experiences have you had?

4. What caused Rachel's death? What was the meaning of the name Rachel gave the newborn son? The meaning of the name Jacob gave the son? Where was Rachel buried? Why do you think she was not buried at the cave of Machpelah?

5. Name the sons of Jacob (35:22-26).

6. Why was Joseph hated by his brothers? Who was most at fault in this? When the brothers decided to harm Joseph, what was their first plan? What was Reuben's plan? What was Judah's plan? How do you think Joseph must have felt during all of this?

7. What made it difficult for the brothers to forget their evil deed?

8. What events in Jacob's life, after his return from Padan-aram, brought him joy? What brought him sorrow?

9. What have you learned about family quarrels from this lesson?

10. Why do you think Scripture records the flaws as well as the virtues of its great personalities?

Perspectives on the Family Crisis

- There is nothing so beautiful as the end of a family quarrel, nor so ugly as the beginning of one.
- Family favoritism fosters friction.
- Parents who deal in deceit ought not to be surprised if their children are good deceivers.
- Jealousy, arrogance, and selfishness, mixed together and baked, produce hatred, divisions, and sorrow.
- "Love is patient and kind; love is not jealous or boastful; it is not arrogant or rude" (1 Corinthians 13:4, RSV).
- Revenge exacts a high price from both the perpetrator and the victim. One sin is never set right by another.
- The bad news of history is the collective record of families gone wrong.

11

Crisis
in Integrity
Genesis 38–41

Before the narrator of Genesis leaves Jacob's family and follows Joseph into Egypt, he relates some sordid events from the life of Judah, one of Jacob's sons by Leah. They reveal some good and bad things about the man through whom would come great kings, particularly the King of kings, Jesus. The events of chapter 38, while casting Judah in an unfavorable light, also serve as a backdrop against which we can view God's special providence in removing Israel's clan from the corruption of Canaan to the haven of Egypt, where they were highly favored for a time.

Integrity Crisis in Canaan
Judah married a Canaanite woman. The first son of this less-than-desirable union was so wicked that God ended his life. According to ancient custom, the second son then had a responsibility to take his dead brother's wife. The first child of this union would be regarded as the child of the departed brother so that his family would not die out. But the second son had no wish to raise up children for his brother. He wanted no children but his own to share the family inheritance. This offense against brotherhood and family caused God to rid the earth of him as well.

Judah then urged the widow, Tamar, to return to her father's house. He promised that his third son, Shelah, would fulfill the family obligation when he became old enough. Tamar waited and watched until she was convinced that Judah was ignoring his promise. We can see that he might be reluctant to keep it. Two of his sons were now dead, and it may have looked to him as if Tamar had something to do with their deaths. Though his own sons were at fault in both cases, he may well have shifted the blame to her. On the other hand, perhaps he meant to keep his promise, but the matter simply was not so important to him as it was to Tamar. A father is apt to be slow to realize that his son has grown up.

When Tamar decided that Judah did not mean to keep his promise, she devised a scheme to expose his duplicity (38:12-30). She dressed herself as a prostitute and stationed herself along a road that she knew Judah was to travel. Giving way to lust, he fell into her trap. Since she wore a harlot's veil, he did not know she was his daughter-in-law. As a price for her sexual favors, Judah promised to send her a young goat from his flock. Shrewd businesswoman that she seemed to be, she asked some guarantee that he would pay his debt. He gave her his signet ring, some bracelets, and his staff. The veiling customs of the time made it possible for her to keep her face covered throughout this affair.

Following their sexual encounter, Tamar returned to her father's house, put off the prostitute's veil, and donned once again the garments that identified her as a widow. Judah, true to his word, sent his friend to pay his debt to the harlot, but he could not find her.

When, in due course, it was learned that Tamar was pregnant, Judah was righteously indignant. He demanded that she be burned alive. Or possibly he ordered that she be burned after being stoned to death. Such a punishment was sometimes given in later times. It seems evident that the head of the family held the power of life or death over family members.

As Tamar was being led to execution, she revealed the identity of the father of her child—the owner of the signet ring, the bracelets, and the staff. It must have been a humiliating moment for Judah. He was about to kill this woman for an offense he himself had fostered. His earlier unfatherly conduct to her also was exposed. He had promised to give her to Shelah, his living son; and he had not kept that promise. As a result of her trick, Judah himself had fathered her child. He now acknowledged his sin, saying, "She hath been more righteous than I; because that I gave her not to Shelah my son."

The incident not only illustrates Judah's hypocrisy and low moral character; it also illuminates well the dangers inherent in intermarriage with the Canaanites. We shall soon see that God removed His people from that danger by leading them to Egypt for a period of some centuries. There He built them into a solidified, God-dependent nation.

But we are getting ahead of our story. The result of this strange union between Judah and Tamar was twin boys, Pharez and Zarah. It was through the line of Pharez that Joseph, Mary's husband, was to come (Matthew 1:3). If Luke traces the descent of Mary, she too was of that line (Luke 3:33). Even in this sordid and sinful affair there is the glimmer of God's ultimate triumph over sin through His only begotten Son.

Integrity Crisis in Egypt

Meanwhile, in Egypt, Jacob's son Joseph faced his own crisis of integrity. Unlike his brother Judah, Joseph met his crisis with dignity and honor.

When they got to Egypt, the members of the spice caravan sold Joseph to Potiphar, the captain of Pharaoh's royal bodyguard. "The Lord greatly blessed Joseph there in the home of his master, so that everything he did succeeded" (39:2, LB). Potiphar learned to have such confidence in this young foreigner that he eventually turned over to him the complete management of his affairs (39:3-6).

Potiphar's high post seems to have required him to be away from home a lot. His lonely wife began to lust after the handsome, capable, intelligent overseer of her husband's business.

Joseph was probably in his mid-twenties when she suggested that he sleep with her. Loyally calling attention to the trust Potiphar had in him, he refused. He clearly saw that the wickedness would not only be against his trusting master, but also against God (39:7-9).

Potiphar's wife was not to be put off easily. Joseph's refusals only increased her lust for him. She continued day after day with her propositioning. Joseph continued with his refusing. Though he tried to stay out of her way as much as possible, she was continually arranging opportunities to invite him to her bed (39:10).

Then came a day when nobody was in the house but the two of them. Demanding again that he go to bed with her, she pulled him toward her. She had undoubtedly made herself quite alluring, using some of the perfumes and cosmetics for which Egypt is famous. Joseph ran for his life, or perhaps we ought to say he ran for his soul. As he tore away from her, she was left holding his outer robe in her hands (39:11, 12).

100

She felt rejected, insulted, and spurned. Her lust turned to hatred. Now she panted for spiteful revenge as much as she had panted for sexual relations. Perhaps she feared that Joseph would expose her to her husband for the unfaithful wife she was.

Retaliating with craftiness, she let out a blood-curdling scream that brought distant servants running into the house. Playing her hysteria scene with dramatic abandon, she told the "big lie" to her startled audience. She charged that Joseph had attempted to seduce or rape her and that only her screams had frightened him away. The robe was *Exhibit A* for the prosecution (39:13-15).

While her "loyal wife" routine played well before the servants, her husband was to be the audience that would really count. She performed before him even better than in her debut before the servants. She warmed to the role with histrionic zeal.

"That Hebrew slave you've had around here," she charged, "tried to rape me, and I was only saved by my screams. He fled, leaving his jacket behind!" (39:16-18, LB). The polished performance had its desired effect. Potiphar went into a rage, and before long Joseph was in prison (39:19, 20).

For all his anger, however, Potiphar treated Joseph rather leniently. Probably he could have had the slave beaten to death. According to Egyptian law, attempted adultery might be punished by more than a thousand blows. Perhaps Potiphar saw through his wife more than he showed.

In whatever case, God was still at work. "But the Lord was with Joseph, and showed him mercy, and gave him favor in the sight of the keeper of the prison" (39:21). Before long, God's favor toward Joseph produced results in Pharaoh's prison just as dramatically as in Potiphar's household. He was given charge of the entire prison administration (39:22, 23).

Joseph's integrity had thrown him from palace to prison. By worldly standards it may seem that Joseph had made a mistake in not giving in to sexual temptation. But far to the contrary, God was preparing him for better things. He had no need to compromise his integrity to gain prosperity "because the Lord was with him, and that which he did, the Lord made it to prosper" (39:23).

From Prison to Power

In Joseph's youth, dreams got him in trouble with his family. Now dreams elevated him from a lowly prison cell to an exalted position in Pharaoh's government.

Pharaoh's cupbearer and his chief baker both fell from favor with the king and were imprisoned in the very place where Joseph had oversight. One night both of them had dreams. They were so disturbed that their faces were downcast the next morning when Joseph came by. When they lamented that there were no soothsayers available to interpret their dreams, Joseph said, "Interpreting dreams is God's business" (40:8, LB).

At Joseph's urging, the cupbearer told him his dream. Joseph interpreted it very favorably for him. In three days his fortunes would turn and he would once again be elevated to his former place in Pharaoh's court (40:9-13). The chief baker, most likely encouraged by the favorable interpretation of his companion's dream, told Joseph his own. The interpretation of this, however, was not at all propitious. While the cupbearer's head would be lifted up by pardon, the baker's head would be lifted off by execution (40:16-19).

It all came about just as God had revealed through Joseph (40:20-22). Joseph asked the cupbearer to intercede for him when he returned to court, but the cupbearer forgot the foreigner he had met in prison (40:14, 15, 23).

Two full years went by with no apparent hope for pardon. Joseph had reason for discouragement. Was he watching and listening each day for word from Pharaoh's palace? Was he disappointed day after day because nothing changed? Was he angry at the forgetfulness of one he had helped? If so, we are not told of it. The Biblical record gives no hint of depression on Joseph's part. Joseph knew that God had not forgotten him even if men had. He merely waited upon God's providence.

Finally, the hand of God moved to jog the cupbearer's memory and create a situation that brought release for Joseph. Pharaoh himself was troubled by two dreams (41:1-8). All the ruler's wise men found themselves unable to interpret the dreams. The light of remembrance, however, at last clicked on in the cupbearer's memory (41:9-13). He recounted to Pharaoh the dreams he and his baker companion had had while in prison, the meeting with the Hebrew who interpreted their dreams, and the fulfillment of the Hebrew's interpretations.

When Pharaoh heard of this dream expert in this unexpected place, he immediately sent for him (41:14). Joseph must certainly have enjoyed the bath, shave, and clean clothing that prepared him for his audience with the most powerful ruler of the land. There must have been a song in his heart and a prayer of thanksgiving on his lips as he stepped out of his prison. He must have wondered at Pharaoh's palace, with its great, soaring columns, high-vaulted ceilings, and ornate entrance ways. He passed through huge outer gates, walked by rows of soldiers, and came before the man who held in his hands the power of great Egypt. If Joseph was awed, we are not told.

Pharaoh got right to the point: "I have dreamed a dream, and there is none that can interpret it: and I have heard say of thee, that thou canst understand a dream to interpret it." Joseph replied, giving glory to God, "It is not in me: God shall give Pharaoh an answer of peace" (41:15, 16).

There had been two dreams, but they both had the same meaning. In one, seven fat and healthy cows came up out of the river, only to be devoured by seven skinny cows. In the second dream, seven full and healthy heads of grain were swallowed by seven withered heads (41:17-24).

The meaning of the dreams was readily apparent to Joseph, led as he was by God. There would be seven years of prosperity in the land of Egypt, but those would be followed by seven years of famine (41:25-32).

Joseph not only interpreted the dreams, but also presumed to make practical suggestions as to a course of action to be taken in light of the interpretation. He suggested that Pharaoh appoint an overseer to supervise preparations for the famine that was to come. This man should establish a bureaucracy to provide government granaries and store a fifth part of the seven good harvests (41:33-36).

This made sense to Pharaoh, who immediately began to sift candidates for the new post of "Secretary of Agriculture." Looking at Joseph, he said, "Can we find such a one as this is, a man in whom the Spirit of God is?" (41:38). The more he thought about it, the more sense it made to him. He said to Joseph, "Forasmuch as God hath showed thee all this, there is none so discreet and wise as thou art: thou shalt be over my house, and according to thy word shall all my people be ruled: only in the throne will I be greater than thou" (41:39, 40).

The king immediately conferred on Joseph symbols of the high office to which he had been appointed. He was given the king's royal signet ring, with its cartouches encircling the king's royal names. A gold chain was put around his neck, and he was sent to the royal tailors for robes of fine linen. He was given a royal chariot from the king's garage, and footmen to proclaim his importance.

Did Joseph ever pinch himself to see if he was dreaming? Pharaoh's favor opened countless doors of service and opportunity for him. Pharaoh conferred on him a new name, Zaphnathpaaneah, "the one who furnishes the nourishment of life." Wherever he went, people bowed in respect or jumped in obedience. For a young man of thirty who had spent seventeen years as a shepherd, perhaps ten as a slave, and three as a jailbird, his new eminence must have been marvelous in the extreme.

For a lesser man than Joseph, this sudden rise in status might have been difficult to handle. He had risen from slave to overseer second only to Pharaoh himself. Catapulted from prison to palace, he suddenly found himself with the sort of power men dream of and die for (41:40, 41).

Pharaoh not only gave Joseph a chariot from the royal car pool, he also gave him a wife from the royal wife pool (41:45). With a gold chain at his neck to show high rank, signet ring on his finger to show authority, and royal linen on his back to show distinction, he set about the task of preparing the land for famine (41:46-49).

Joseph proved himself equal to the confidence Pharaoh placed in him. During the years of plenty, he gathered and stored until there was so much that the exact count was lost. His days were filled with significant responsibility. In addition to integrity, he must have had executive ability of a high order.

When his first son was born, Joseph called him Manasseh, "causing to forget." This called attention to the marvelous way God had made up to him for the loss of home and freedom. The second son, Ephraim, was named "fruitful" in thanks to God for His blessing that had made Joseph fruitful in this foreign land (41:50-52).

When the seven years of plenty ended, Egypt was well prepared for the days of famine. The Egyptian officials must have watched carefully the nilometers at Aswan, checking constantly on the fluctuations of the flow of that great river upon which Egypt so greatly depended. The day came, in due course, when it was observed that the river was not rising as it ought. God had limited the rains in the mountains from which the Nile draws its waters. Joseph, who had been in charge of accumulating and storing, now became the supervisor of rationing. He oversaw the distribution of relief supplies that Egyptians and foreigners sought to buy. By controlling the food supply in a time of extreme famine, Joseph held power of life and death for those who came before him. It is a measure of his trust in God that he was not corrupted by such power (41:53-57).

It is worth noting that in whatever condition he found himself, Joseph never ceased to think and talk about God. In his confrontation with a wicked woman, he talked about God (39:9); in his confinement in prison, he talked about God (40:8); in the court of Pharaoh, he talked about God (41:16); and later, among his brothers, he talked about God (42:18; 45:5-8).

Such talk was no afterthought for Joseph. It was the first thing on his lips. Joseph confessed God not only with his lips, but also with his trusting, honorable life. It is no wonder that his crises inevitably turned into victories.

In the two instances noted in this chapter, we have seen contrasts in integrity. Judah, forgetful and immoral, did not live up to his word. He was humiliated when the truth about his conduct became known. Joseph, in contrast, was honest and above board. He trusted in God no matter what the circumstances of his life. Wherever he found himself, God blessed him. His life was filled with the most cruel of disappointments, but he knew that through all these vicissitudes God was at work for his good. He approached life with a sense that, despite his surroundings, he was always God's man. He refused to compromise for personal pleasure or advantage. He saw that sexual sin with his master's wife was not only sin against a person who was his friend and benefactor, but also an offense against God. He realized that whatever wisdom he had in the interpretation of dreams was given him by God. It was God who orchestrated the dreams, gave the interpretations, and worked the interpretations for his good. He remained as honest in his high position as he had been in his low estate. He was a man who was as unlikely to use prosperity and power for personal advantage as he was to strike for his advantage when he had nothing. How we need men and women like Joseph in public life, in positions of responsibility of all kinds throughout our society—people who cannot be bought, who will not compromise their integrity, come what may!

Joseph was not a believer in situation ethics. He was a believer in God, who judges all man's actions with justice and truth. If ever there was a man who could have rationalized rebellion, bitterness, and resentment, it was Joseph. Yet there was a particular sweetness about his attitudes and strength about his character that all responded to.

Each day we face crises of integrity. In them we cast our lot either with God or with the ways of man. Would that we might learn the lesson of God's love and care for Joseph.

For Reflection

1. What evidence do we have in Genesis 38 that Judah was not the kind of man he ought to have been?

2. What kind of sons did Judah have?

3. What good fortune came to Joseph upon his arrival in Egypt? What was the cause of his success? (39:2, 3).

4. After Joseph rose to responsibility in Potiphar's house, what ended his service there? What were his reasons for not sinning? (39:9).

5. What was prison like for Joseph? What special people did he meet there? What dreams did he interpret? Why was he able to do this?

6. How did Joseph move from prison to a high position in government? Describe Pharaoh's two dreams and Joseph's interpretation.

7. Why do you think Pharaoh was so quick to put this relatively unknown young man into a position of such great authority? If their paths crossed, as they must have, what do you think was Potiphar's reaction to all this?

8. What do we learn about integrity from this lesson?

9. What do we learn about reacting to injustice, malice, and spite?

10. If Joseph were alive today and were asked to speak to a group of Christians about the things he learned in the course of his life, what do you think he would say?

Perspectives on the Integrity Crisis

• It is better to be in prison for faithfulness than to be in a palace with a guilty conscience.

• God is the basis of moral principles. We are to be holy because He is holy (1 Peter 1:16). Adultery is not merely an offense against a man or a woman; it is an offense against God.

• It is better to lose a robe and a job than to lose a soul.

• "The righteousness of the blameless will smooth his way, but the wicked will fall by his own wickedness" (Proverbs 11:5, NASB).

12

Crisis
in Love
Genesis 42–44

Famine

Famine was in the land—emaciating, wrenching, terrifying famine! Irrigation canals were dry in Egypt. The hot east wind lifted into the air the powder dust of formerly luxuriant fields. Animals were walking skeletons. The countryside was littered with decaying carcasses. Death stalked the land. In Egypt, however, there was hope. Joseph had prepared the land for this terrible ordeal. The granaries were full.

In Hebron things were not so hopeful. Jacob, unlike Pharaoh, had received no warning. Things had gone along as usual during good years of harvest. But now starvation and want were everywhere—everywhere, that is, but in Egypt. Rumor of Egypt's abundance reached the concerned patriarch who saw with mounting concern impending catastrophe. Finally he could put off decisive action no longer. He called his sons together, put money in their hands, and sent them to Egypt in hopes of buying enough grain there to stave off impending ruin and death (42:1-3).

All of Jacob's sons set out on the journey except Benjamin, the youngest, who was probably now in his early twenties. Benjamin, like Joseph before him, was his father's favorite. The old man was not willing that he be subjected to danger (42:4). Was Jacob suspicious and distrustful of his other sons? Was he less than completely satisfied with the story these sons had told of the death of Joseph? Or was he only thinking of the natural dangers of travel, particularly in a time when people were desperate for survival? We cannot know for sure. But it is clear that this son, born through the death of Jacob's most beloved wife, was extremely precious to him. His other sons, apparently, took this for granted. There is no evidence of jealousy such as they had felt toward Joseph.

The sons of Jacob joined the hordes of desperate people on the trails to Egypt. They looked not unlike the others whose faces were drawn in fear and desperation. Little did they know, as they entered the land of the Nile, the chain of events their coming was to set in motion.

Joseph was in charge of the distribution of the supplies that Pharaoh was making available to foreigners. It took a man of firmness and fairness. It must have been a difficult task, human nature being what it is. There must have come before him those who saw the famine as a business opportunity. They came to buy as much as they could in order to profit from the misery of the time. They exaggerated their needs and had no concern for the starving. There came others who were on the brink of death, but who had little money or cattle with which to buy what they needed. There were times when Joseph needed to be hard, and times when he needed to be compassionate. He watched people carefully, reading their motives, listening, and making judgments.

There must have been apprehension in the hearts of the ten brothers from Hebron as they joined the bread line in Egypt. As they moved slowly toward the Egyptian government officials who were distributing the food, they must have asked others around them what was going on: "Do you think there will be enough for us all?" "What is the going rate for a bushel of grain?" "How do the Egyptians decide how much each person is to get?" "What kind of person is the man in charge?" "Does he ever turn anyone away empty-handed?" "How much do you hope to get?" "What is the situation in your part of the country?" "How long do you think the famine will last?" "Do you know of anywhere else besides Egypt where there is grain for sale?" "What do you expect to do if we get no rain for next year's crops?" It must have been a cosmopolitan crowd, gossiping, worrying, waiting, wondering. Egyptians watched over the crowd, quick to settle any unruliness. The wait seemed interminable. It was difficult to be patient. So much rested on the outcome of their interview with the Egyptian officials in charge. Jacob's brothers squatted, stood, paced, reclined, and slept as their little section of the slowly advancing line moved forward.

When, finally, their turn came, the ten brothers stood before Joseph. He immediately recognized them as the men who had sold him into slavery about twenty years before. They, however, did not recognize this influential man speaking the tongue of Egypt and wearing Egyptian linen (42:5-8). As they bowed before him with their faces to the earth, Joseph's mind must have gone back to that dream that had so infuriated them (42:9). Their sheaves were bowing down to his, just as the dream had predicted (37:7).

Fear

Joseph spoke to them roughly, "Where do you come from? What do you really want?" If their wait had increased their fear of this exalted ruler who held in his hands the power of life and death for all of them, his accusations must have struck terror to their hearts. He accused them of being enemy agents, come to spy out the weakness of Egypt (42:9).

They protested that their only reason for coming to Egypt was to buy food. They were just an ordinary family—honest, hard-working, true (42:10, 11). To impress the governor, who continued to accuse them of being spies, they gave details of their family: twelve sons of one man in Canaan, one son still with the father, one son dead. Little did they realize that this was not totally new information to the man who accused them (42:13).

Joseph, continuing to test their veracity, proposed that they prove to him that their story was not merely a "cover." He would believe them, he declared, only if they could produce this youngest brother of whom they spoke. Further, he would believe their story only if that youngest brother could be brought to Egypt. One of them, he proposed, could go back and get him while the others remained in custody in Egypt (42:15, 16). They had little choice, for otherwise they would be treated as spies by Pharaoh's men. That was not a happy prospect.

Joseph had succeeded in getting their attention. To allow time for contemplation, he put them all in jail for three days. By comparison to Joseph's own imprisonment, this was a short stay indeed. But it must have been extremely harrowing for his ten brothers who fretted about what should be done. Then the Egyptian himself supplied the solution—instead of keeping many and sending one, he would keep one and send many. Attributing his magnanimous decision to his fear of God, the Egyptian proposed that one of them be left behind as surety while the others returned to their country with the purpose of bringing back the corroboration of their story, their youngest brother (42:17-20).

Joseph noted carefully their reactions to this proposal. While offering freedom to the majority, it nevertheless meant that one brother would remain in custody. Would this decision about who would stay bring out the worst in his brothers? Instead of selfishness and division, Joseph observed remorse. They did not know that Joseph, who had constantly used a translator, could understand them as they connected their present difficulty to their past sin, saying, "We are verily guilty concerning our brother, in that we saw the anguish of his soul, when he besought us, and we would not hear; therefore is this distress come upon us" (42:21).

For about twenty years they had been carrying the burden of guilt for their treatment of Joseph. One wonders if that guilt haunted them in every difficulty that came their way during all those years. Reuben, in particular, spoke out, reminding them that they should have listened to him when he protested against their evil actions with Joseph. Now, he pointed out, they were finally paying the price for their sin (42:22).

Their admission of guilt brought tears to Joseph's eyes, tears that he attempted to conceal from them. His brothers seemed sorry for their sin against him, but sorrow and repentance are not necessarily the same thing. There remained the necessity for further testing of these men. It still remained to be seen whether or not they had actually changed. Thus Joseph proceeded with his plan.

Was it out of remembrance of Reuben's efforts to save his life that Joseph chose Simeon, the second eldest son, to bind and keep behind (42:24)? Or was it respect for Reuben's role as the leader of this journeying band of Hebrews who were about to continue a hazardous journey? With famine in the land, those transporting food were subject to constant danger.

The nine sons of Jacob at length set out toward home, well supplied with sacks of grain. But when, on the trail, one of them opened his bag to feed his donkey, he discovered an unsettling thing. He found in the sack the money that he had paid the Egyptians for the grain. It was a very disconcerting, frightening, and mystifying thing for this Hebrew band of travelers. While they did not know what to make of it, they perceived that behind all that was happening to them there was the hand of God (42:28).

Frustration

Arriving home, they recounted to their father all the strange things that had happened in Egypt. They spoke of the governor's insistence that they prove their veracity by returning with their youngest brother, and of Simeon whom they had left behind. Then, as they opened the precious sacks of grain that they had brought back from Egypt, they discovered that *each* sack contained the purchase money with the grain. Talk about fear! Now everyone was shaking—sons and father alike (42:35). If they went again to Egypt, would they be accused of stealing?

Jacob, however, was not willing to hazard his beloved son, Benjamin, in this strange affair. Joseph, the other of Rachel's sons, was gone. Simeon, his second son, was being held captive in a foreign land. He could not help thinking that all this bode ill for Benjamin as well. Reuben, making the greatest offer of assurance he could make to his troubled father, proferred his own two sons as pledges for Benjamin. Still Jacob refused to let Benjamin go. "If anything happens to him," the old man said, "I'll die" (42:36-38).

What reason, persuasion, and promises could not accomplish, hunger did. When all the grain of those precious sacks was gone, it was obvious that another trip to Egypt was inevitable.

Judah explained to his still reluctant father that they could not return to the land of the Nile without Benjamin. There was absolutely no other way for them to go successfully before the great Egyptian overseer (43:1-5). Jacob kicked a tent pole, wrung his hands, and, for the thousandth time, said, "Why? Why did you tell that man you have another brother? What difference does that make to him?" Patiently, the sons again explained to their distraught father that the Egyptian had asked about their family and that they had had no reason to believe that truthfulness was going to work against them. Who could have anticipated that the Egyptian would think them spies, or that he would demand that they bring their youngest brother back with them to authenticate their story? (43:6, 7).

When Judah persisted in his urging, and it became obvious that all of the family would die if something were not done soon, Jacob reluctantly gave in. Judah did his best to reassure the old man, pledging himself to guarantee with his own life Benjamin's safety (43:8, 9). He was not, however, above voicing a few recriminations of his own. The whole sorry business, he told his father, would have long since been behind them had not Jacob delayed and been so stubborn in letting Benjamin go (43:10).

111

For all his hesitancy in the face of imminent disaster, Jacob was still the wise trader and businessman of old. He determined that his sons should offer the best presents they could take from their famine-torn land—balm, honey, myrrh, almonds, and other nuts and spices (43:11). Assuming that the returned money of the former trip must have been a mistake, he sent with his sons double money for their new purchases. Thus his sons could stand honorably before this hard governor the old patriarch had heard so much about (43:12).

Finally Jacob entrusted to the care of his sons his most precious possession, the only remaining son of Rachel, the son who had been born as his mother had died. With stoical resignation, the old man committed the matter to God and once again sent his sons on their way (43:13, 14). We can only wonder at the feelings of this aged patriarch as he saw his sons set out—all of his sons this time. They were moving toward a land which offered life in the form of food, but which was filled with danger and possible death for those he loved. Finally he ceased to struggle against the inevitable. "What is to be, will be," he may have thought. "If I be bereaved of my children, I am bereaved" (43:14).

Accusation

Arriving back in Egypt, Jacob's sons again found themselves before the great overseer who had so complicated their lives with his suspicions and demands. They were perplexed the more when he invited them to his home for lunch. Something awfully sinister was afoot, they were sure. Could it be that this governor was going to punish them because of the money that had mysteriously appeared in their grain sacks? Could it be that he was leading them into a trap with the intention of taking all they had and selling them into slavery? (43:18). (These fears represented a certain poetic justice in light of what they had done to Joseph.)

While they awaited the arrival of the governor, they nervously queried Joseph's steward, pouring out like a torrent all their fears. They were, they asserted over and over again, innocent in the matter of the money, regardless of the circumstantial evidenced *sacked* against them (43:19-22).

The steward, perhaps forcing back a smile, assured them that the money transaction on their last trip was satisfactory and that they could stop trembling. He said, "Peace be to you, fear not: your God, and the God of your father, hath given you treasure in your sacks: I had your money" (43:23). Had they been listening attentively here, they might have caught this small clue that things were other than they seemed. It is interesting that the servant spoke so knowingly about the God of their father. It seems that those closest to Joseph had come to know that great sovereign God for themselves. Joseph, as we have noted, constantly talked about God. We need not think that his power and prestige had changed that. His Egyptian servant, it seems, was no longer a stranger to the God of Abraham, Isaac, and Israel. If Jacob's sons noticed this with curiosity, they had no time to follow up on it with further questions of the steward. They were too overjoyed when he brought in their brother Simeon, the brother that had been held as surety for their return.

As they awaited the arrival of the exalted master of the house, the servant saw to it that the feet of Jacob's sons were washed and that their donkeys were provided with food. They must have marveled at the opulence of this Egyptian household, with its painted walls, elaborate furniture, and fine appointments. These men of tents had doubtless never been in anything quite like it. They very carefully laid out their presents—the spices and nuts that they had brought—so that the governor would see them immediately upon his arrival at midday. How ordinary and provincial these small tokens of respect must have seemed as they lay there amidst the wealth of the Egyptian household! Yet, myrrh was highly prized in this land of mummies and perhaps, just perhaps, the gifts might soften the heart of this enigmatic governor.

It was noon when Joseph came, perhaps arriving in his royal chariot, accompanied by a fan bearer. It was confirmed to Jacob's sons that the Egyptian expected them to be his guests for the meal. They presented their gifts with as much ceremony as these comparatively uncultured men could muster, bowing low in respect before the governor (43:26). (Shades of the sheaves.)

With what must have seemed to them mere oriental solicitude, the prince asked about their health and the health of their father. Joseph's eyes paid little attention to these men, and even less to the presents they had brought. His were on Benjamin, his brother. He just could not take his eyes off the son in whose delivery his mother had died. If Jacob's sons had been listening closely, they might have heard a quiver in Joseph's voice as he said to this young man before him, "God be gracious unto thee, my son" (43:29). If they had been truly observant, they would have seen the tears welling up in the ruler's eyes as he made a quick exit to weep unobserved.

When the prince returned, his emotions now under control and his face washed clean of tears, he commanded that the meal be served. As the Egyptian custom demanded, the Hebrews ate by themselves, not at the same table with the Egyptians of Joseph's household. Though they did not recognize it, the Hebrews were given another clue as to the identity of this prince with whom they were eating. They were seated at the table according to their ages, a fact that perplexed but did not enlighten them (43:32, 33). Joseph must have smiled a little as they marveled at his knowledge of them, speculating that this Egyptian host most certainly had powers of knowledge beyond their ken.

Joseph, perhaps seeking to observe the brothers' reactions, showed obvious favoritism to Benjamin. The youngest was given five times as much food as anyone else. This obvious partiality seemed not to disturb the others who, loosened by food and drink, relaxed and truly enjoyed themselves. "They had a wonderful time bantering back and forth, and the wine flowed freely!" (43:34, LB).

Apprehension

The following day, as they goaded their overloaded donkeys home toward Hebron, Jacob's sons were doubtless reliving the great good time of the governor's banquet. Things had gone very well, very well indeed. They were *all* on their way home with filled stomachs and filled sacks. The hard governor had turned out to be a most amiable fellow, once they got to know him. All Jacob's living sons, according to their knowledge at least, were once again united and headed for the safety of home. Judah, who had taken responsibility for young Benjamin, must have been particularly pleased. The trials were over at last, so he thought (44:1-3).

Then suddenly Joseph's steward and his deputies, revolving lights blinking on their camels, pulled them over. The charge was grand theft. Someone had stolen the governor's silver cup, and they were prime suspects. While the brothers protested their innocence, the steward read them their rights: no one would be charged unless he was caught with the hot goods (44:10).

A quick shakedown of the caravan revealed the hot cup in young Benjamin's sack (44:11, 12). Benjamin knew that he had been framed, and so did the steward; but the brothers had no way of knowing whom to believe. Poor Judah was apoplectic. In a gesture of despair, he and the others tore their clothes in humiliation and sorrow.

With great anguish, they returned to the house where they had enjoyed such gracious hospitality. Before the governor, they fell to the ground (those sheaves, again). The governor stared at them in anger. "What in the world were you trying to do?" he shouted. "Didn't you know that a person of my powers would know what you were doing?" (44:15).

Judah, who had taken responsibility for Benjamin when they left home for Egypt, spoke for all the men. He pleaded "no contest." There was no plausible defense for him to adopt. There was no way to clear the name of the family. Judah recognized that Benjamin had been found with the stolen property. But more than that, he recognized in their present distress the judgment of God on his iniquity and that of his brothers for their sins against Joseph (44:16). Judah, his spirit bowed down, resigned himself and the others to perpetual slavery to this governor whom they had so wickedly wronged.

"Not so," the governor said, in effect. "The innocent will go free. I need only prosecute the guilty party. The rest of you can go back to your father" (44:17).

Here was the moment of decision. Would these brothers once again turn on one of Rachel's sons in an act of self-interest? Would they gladly act in such a way as to be rid of another of their father's favorites? Now their love for their father and for one another would be seen for what it really was, whether for good or for evil.

Judah spoke for them all. He recounted the events that had brought them to this tragic moment, speaking tenderly of his old father and respectfully of Jacob's special love for the child of his old age, Benjamin. He spoke of the reluctance of their father to part with the young man and their present fear that their return without the boy would most certainly mean the death of the old patriarch.

Judah recounted too the sorrow Jacob had felt over the loss of his other son by Rachel, the one presumed torn by wild beasts. Judah told of his promise of surety for the safety of Benjamin. Finally, he humbly petitioned the governor to permit him to take Benjamin's place and to suffer whatever penalty the boy's crime deserved (44:18-34).

The love of Judah for his father was genuine and moving. Judah was willing, in self-sacrificing love, to give up his own life and liberty for his brother. He had come a long way from the days when he suggested that they sell Joseph for twenty pieces of silver.

The trial was now over. Far more than confession of guilt, it was these words of family love that Joseph had longed to hear. Tears

115

welling up in his eyes, Joseph ordered all his Egyptian attendants to leave. Then he broke into sobs that echoed through the palace.

Then came three words from the governor—three words that startled Jacob's sons—three words that filled them with joy, and with terror: "I am Joseph" (45:3).

Besides Joseph, Judah is the major hero of this section of Scripture. It is he who eloquently expresses his deep love for his father and who is willing to take on himself the punishment of another. He meets his test of love by laying himself down in sacrifice. In this he is much like his descendant, Jesus, who lovingly laid down His life for the sins of mankind.

For Reflection

1. When Joseph's brothers first appeared in Egypt, what accusation did Joseph make against them? How did he propose that they prove their integrity?

2. When Joseph's brothers found themselves in trouble, what did they think was the reason? (42:21).

3. How did Jacob feel about sending Benjamin to Egypt with his brothers? Why did he finally change his mind?

4. What kind of a reception did Joseph give the brothers when they arrived in Egypt the second time?

5. How did Joseph test the brothers to see if their attitude had changed in the years since they had sold him as a slave? What was the result of the test? What had caused them to change?

6. Do you think Joseph was cruel or vindictive in his treatment of his brothers? What would you have done if you had been in his place?

7. What does this record teach us about a guilty conscience? About love? Would you describe Joseph's love for his family as "tough love"? Why?

8. What part did God play in the events we have considered in this chapter and the one before it? What purposes of God were served by what happened?

9. What wrong actions really helped to accomplish God's purposes? Does that make the wrong actions right?

10. What can we take from this study and apply in our relationships with others? What mistakes can we avoid? What examples can we follow?

Perspectives on the Love Crisis

• Judah grew a lot. He finally came to the place where he would rather be a slave himself than inflict slavery on a brother.
• What Joseph did to his brothers and his aging father may seem, at first glance, to be cruel. But it was part of the process of their repentance. When trouble came, they searched their lives for guilt and felt remorse for their wrongdoing.
• When evil threatened them, Joseph's brothers were sure it was the punishment of God. You cannot outrun a guilty conscience.
• "Greater love hath no man than this, that a man lay down his life for his friends" (John 15:13).

13

Crisis

in Reconciliation
Genesis 45–50

Recognition

It was truly a moment of recognition when Joseph was sure of the change in Judah and his brothers. They showed both self-sacrificing love for their father and tender concern for their youngest brother. Such love and concern had been notably lacking in their relationship with Joseph in earlier years. Recognizing the change, Joseph broke into tears as he identified himself to his startled brothers.

Their recognition of Joseph brought fear and consternation. They drew back in terror. In front of them stood that governor, second only to Pharaoh in power and authority. That governor had first treated them roughly, then had treated them graciously. More recently they had been trembling for their lives before him because of the silver cup found in Benjamin's food sack. The Egyptian was still dressed the same. He still was the governor, with all the symbols of his authority. But he no longer used his translator. He was speaking to them in their own language, saying, "I am Joseph."

If attention of the brothers was riveted on the governor, the governor's mind was on his elderly father. "Does my father yet live?" he asked (45:3). It was no longer "your father" that he was talking about (43:27). Now it was "my father." What a difference!

The brothers were speechless, stunned by what they heard. They had fearfully returned to stand accused of theft before this man, but they had come with clear consciences, not really knowing how it was that the silver cup had come into their possession. Now they stood in fear, guilty in heart and conscience of a crime much worse even than theft.

With recognition of Joseph came renewed recognition of their guilt before him, before their father, and before God himself. They had terribly misused this man who now held them in the palm of his hand. It is not surprising that they were "troubled at his presence" (45:3).

Joseph recognized their need to be reassured. Their sin had brought separation, but Joseph's mind was on reconciliation. He reached out to them in love: "Come near to me, I pray you" (45:4).

He spoke to them with soothing and reassuring words. Earlier Joseph had noted their remorse for their sin against him (42:21-23; 44:16). He wanted them to know that he could do what their own guilty consciences could not do: he could forgive them. Rather than blaming his brothers for what had befallen him, Joseph praised God. Joseph saw that what had happened was God's gracious provision for the children of promise. He had been sent ahead to prepare the way for them (45:5-8).

Joseph recognized too that it was God, not his own cleverness, that had exalted him to a position where he managed the whole of Egypt (45:8).

Joseph urged his brothers to return to Jacob with the news of Joseph's power in Egypt and of Pharaoh's invitation for Jacob, his clan, and his possessions to come into Egypt to settle in Goshen, a land good for their flocks and herds of cattle (45:9-13).

Reunion

It must have been quite a reunion, after the first shock of recognition wore off. When the brothers finally realized that Joseph bore them no ill will, they found their voices again and were able to talk freely with him—tears, hugs, remembrances, talk, joy (45:14, 15).

Pharaoh too was pleased with the happy reunion. He urged Joseph to supply his brothers with wagons to transport the Hebrew women, children, and elderly from Canaan to their new home in Egypt (45:16-21). The brothers soon found themselves wearing new robes of finest Egyptian craftsmanship. To Benjamin, his only full brother, Joseph gave five changes of clothing and three hundred pieces of silver. To his father, he sent ten donkey loads of food. Ten other donkeys carried other "good things of Egypt" (45:22, 23). It was an impressive caravan that moved out toward Canaan, where Jacob was waiting anxiously.

Joseph's parting words to his brothers as they set out for home again were, "Don't quarrel along the way!" (45:24, LB). Was this stern warning or ironic humor? In either case, they undoubtedly got the point. Joseph certainly hoped that by now his brothers had learned their lesson about family quarrels.

The homeward trek must have been a mixture of excitement, relief, amazement, and anxiety for Joseph's brothers. On the one hand, they surely felt relieved that Joseph was not dead and that he seemed to hold them no grudge. On the other, they still had to face up to their guilt before their father. Did they spend some of the time on the trail rehearsing their first words to Jacob? How could they tell him? Would his old heart be able to take the news? What would he think when he found out the whole truth about what they had done to Joseph?

When his returning sons spoke of a son who had returned, as it were, from the dead, Jacob could scarcely believe his ears. It was too good to be true! But when he saw all the wagons and provisions that Joseph had sent, his eyes widened and his heart beat with joy (45:25-27). Jacob now had a mission in life. He would see that lost son if it was the last thing he did (45:28).

Reaffirmation

As Jacob and his retinue moved slowly south toward the land of the Nile, a familiar thing happened. God spoke to Jacob. He had spoken before when Jacob was fleeing from Canaan toward Haran. Then he had been escaping from a vengeful brother threatening to take his life. Now he was escaping from a land that threatened his life with famine and death. Then he had been fleeing from a bitter brother; now he was moving toward a loving son.

The old man may have needed reassurance that what he was doing was right. He paused at Beersheba, the place where Isaac had offered sacrifices and had received a message from God (26:23-25). There Jacob made sacrifices of his own (46:1). There in the night he saw a vision. In the vision God approved of his entrance into Egypt, promising to be with him there. God had forbidden Isaac to go there during a previous famine (26:1-5), but now it was time for Isaac's son to go. God also renewed the covenant promise: He would make of Jacob a great nation (46:3). Thus reassured, Jacob went cheerfully on his way (46:5-7).

Pausing in the narrative here, the writer of Genesis lists the names of the family members who went down into Egypt. Sixty-six of Jacob's descendants went with him (46:26). Jacob himself made the number of travelers sixty-seven. With Joseph and his two sons, the family included seventy in all (46:27). This family would grow into a nation and would return, God said (46:3, 4). He had made the same promise to Abraham many years before (15:13, 14).

Reception

Joseph, with the approval of Pharaoh, made arrangements for Jacob to settle in Goshen (46:28-34). What a glorious meeting there must have been between father and son! (46:29, 30).

Some time later, Joseph appeared before Pharaoh with five of his brothers and with his father. Pharaoh received them amiably, welcoming them to Goshen, where they could pasture their flocks unmolested (47:1-6). When Pharaoh asked Jacob his age, the old man replied, "The days of the years of my pilgrimage are hundred and thirty years: few and evil have the days of the years of my life been" (47:9). His early years had certainly been filled with turmoil and deceit, but now he was approaching the end of his faith pilgrimage with honor and dignity.

While Jacob's clan had been rescued from the ravages of drought (47:11, 12), many others had not been so fortunate. As the famine continued, people of Egypt flocked to buy from Pharaoh's grain stores. When their money ran out, they traded their cattle, sheep, goats, horses, and donkeys for the precious grain. When the livestock was gone, they sold their land. Finally, they sold themselves (47:13-23). Massive relocation projects were undertaken (47:21) as Pharaoh more and more consolidated his power over his people.

The people, despite their personal losses, were grateful to the ruler for saving their lives. They hoped that someday soon they might again be able to grow sufficient crops. They besought Pharaoh for seed grain for planting, which he supplied with the understanding that he would receive one-fifth of the produce (47:23-26).

Return

Meanwhile, in Goshen, things went well for the descendants of Jacob. The old man must have been pleased as he saw his people prospering and as he saw the respect given to his son in this sophisticated, cultured land. For seventeen years, he and his were happy in Goshen (47:27, 28).

Then, as he saw his death approaching, the patriarch called his famous son to him and made a last request: "Please bury me in the family burying place in Hebron." The prince of Egypt assured him that this final respect would be done (47:29-31).

To recognize Joseph's special place among his sons, Jacob gave a special distinction to Joseph's sons, Ephraim and Manasseh. Jacob claimed these two as his, thus making these two grandsons equal with his sons. Joseph's family would have two shares of the family wealth and privilege.

Jacob, now nearly blind, called these two young men to him to give them his blessing. In a scene that must have taken his mind back through the corridors of memory to the deception he had perpetrated on his own blind father, Jacob drew his grandsons to him, hugging and kissing them. Then, placing his hands on their heads, he prepared to pronounce the patriarchal blessing.

However, he placed his right hand on the head of the younger and his left on the head of the older. Joseph thought this must be accidental. He hurried to correct his father's mistake before the blessing was given. But Jacob insisted that he was doing just what he meant to do. As the right hand indicated, the younger brother would be greater than the older (48:19). Later history showed that this was a true prophecy, not just a wish of Jacob. This was the fourth time in the line of the patriarchs that a younger son was preferred over an older one. Isaac was preferred over Ishmael, Jacob over Esau, Joseph over Reuben, and Ephraim over Manasseh.

Jacob's blessing rang with his great faith in God. "God," he said, "before whom my fathers Abraham and Isaac did walk, the God which fed me all my life long unto this day, the angel which redeemed me from all evil, bless the lads; and let my name be named on them, and the name of my fathers Abraham and Isaac; and let them grow into a multitude in the midst of the earth" (48:15, 16).

Finally Jacob gathered all his sons around him to pronounce his blessing on each of them (49). Judah's blessing stands out among them (49:8-12). "The sceptre," Jacob said, "shall not depart from Judah, nor a lawgiver from between his feet, until Shiloh come; and unto him shall the gathering of the people be" (49:10). Here we see the glimmer of Messianic prophecy, for Jesus would be born through this kingly line.

When Jacob finished, he renewed his request to be buried with Abraham, Sarah, Isaac, Rebekah, and Leah. Then he lay back on his bed and quietly died (49:29-33).

Joseph, now the undisputed leader of the sons of Jacob, took charge of the funeral arrangements. Jacob's body was handed over to the Egyptian embalmers for forty days. The Egyptians, joining the Hebrews in their sorrow, mourned the departed patriarch for seventy days (50:1-3). Then Joseph asked Pharaoh's permission to fulfill his father's wish to be buried in Canaan (50:4-6).

Pharaoh assented and sent along with the funeral party a great company of servants, chariots, and horsemen. (The Egyptians, as we have come to know, were accustomed to extremely elaborate funeral arrangements. The Great Pyramid of Cheops was probably around 750 years old at the time of Jacob's death.) Jacob, out of deference to Joseph, was treated by the Egyptians with the honor and ceremony deemed appropriate for the burial of a great man (50:7-11). His sons carried the mummy to its final resting place, the cave of Machpelah, where Jacob was buried with tenderness and love (50:12, 13).

Renewal

As the burial party turned to begin its return to Egypt, Joseph's brothers were frightened. What might befall them now that their father was gone? Might Joseph seek a vengeance he had held in abeyance during the life of their father? Wise to the ways of human wrath, they simply couldn't believe that Joseph would not eventually move to get even with them (50:14, 15).

Fearing to stand before Joseph's face, they sent a messenger to ask forgiveness. Before his death, the messenger said, Jacob had urged them to seek Joseph's forgiveness, saying, "Forgive, I pray thee now, the trespass of thy brethren, and their sin; for they did unto thee evil: and now, we pray thee, forgive the trespass of the servants of the God of thy father." When he heard these words, Joseph burst into tears (50:17).

Joseph had not changed. Never, it seems, did the idea of revenge enter his mind. As tears came to his eyes at the words of their humble request, Joseph's mind must once again have returned to the dream of his youth as the brothers "fell down before his face; and they said, Behold, we be thy servants" (50:18).

Joseph understood a very important principle: "Vengeance is mine; I will repay, saith the Lord" (Romans 12:19). He harbored no bitterness. What they had intended for evil, God had used for good. If God had used even their offense for a good purpose, how could Joseph blame anyone? (50:19, 20).

Reconciliation

Joseph not only promised forgiveness, he also promised favor (50:21). Far from seeking revenge, he offered reassurance, sustenance, comfort, and love.

From that point on the years passed quickly. We are told very little of the remaining fifty-four years of Joseph's life (50:22-26). They must have been years of glory and honor.

Though Egypt was good to him and his, Joseph was not forgetful of God's promises to Abraham, Isaac, and Jacob. Egypt had been his adopted home, but it was not the home of promise. The bones of his fathers lay in Canaan, and he himself looked forward to the day when his own bones would rest beside theirs.

Joseph knew that God would bring His people out of Egypt one day (50:24). When he died at 110, his body was embalmed and laid in a coffin. During all the days that were to follow—the days of captivity and the days of deliverance—that solitary mummy was to be a reminder that the day of exodus would come and that God's nation would once again dwell in the land promised to Abraham, Isaac, and Israel (50:25, 26; Exodus 13:19).

For Reflection

1. Why do you think Pharaoh had such a friendly attitude toward Jacob and his family? How did he express his favor?

2. What was Jacob's reaction to the news that Joseph still lived?

3. In what ways had the days of Jacob's life been "evil"? In what ways had they been good?

4. What happened to the Egyptians who needed grain from the government stores as the famine continued? What effect did this continuing famine have on the power structure in Egypt?

5. What promise did Jacob seek from Joseph before he died? How did Jacob elevate the family of Joseph? What was unusual about the blessings given to Ephraim and Manasseh?

6. Why were Joseph's brothers fearful after Jacob's death? What did they do to bring peace? What did Joseph say and do to reassure them?

7. When his own death approached, what arrangements did Joseph make for his burial?

8. What do you learn about forgiveness and reconciliation from this study of Joseph and his brothers?

9. How does Genesis 50:20 apply to your life as you face problems and difficulties? Do you recall times when good resulted from what seemed bad?

10. If Egypt was so good to Joseph and his relatives, why were they so attached to Canaan that both Jacob and Joseph wanted to be buried there?

Perspectives on the Forgiveness Crisis

• God can bring good from things that men and women do out of evil motives.

• It is sometimes just as difficult to accept forgiveness as it is to give it.

• "For if ye forgive men their trespasses, your heavenly Father will also forgive you: but if ye forgive not men their trespasses, neither will your Father forgive your trespasses" (Matthew 6:14, 15).

• Joseph was not like many of us who pretend to forgive while we continue to hold our grudges.

The Continuing Crisis

We have come to the end of Genesis, but the story of crisis continues. As the physical and spiritual descendants of these strugglers, we have our own moments of decision to face. We too face decisions related to purpose and identity, freedom and responsibility, brotherhood and faith, trust and doubt, obedience and self-interest, relationships and family, integrity and trust, and love and reconciliation.

We have witnessed the victories and defeats of these men and women of the past; they too may be witnessing ours. After speaking in chapter 11 of the greats of the faith, the writer of Hebrews begins chapter 12 by noting that in our spiritual races we are surrounded by a great crowd of "witnesses." These observers, it seems, are those whose lives have borne witness to the providence and love of God. We are bound in eternal fellowship with them.

These also, one and all, are commemorated for their faith; and yet they did not enter upon the promised inheritance, because, with us in mind, God had made a better plan, that only in company with us should they reach their perfection.
—Hebrews 11:39, NEB

We have seen that those who met the crises of their lives with victory were people who trusted in the promises of God and who were obedient to the commands of God. Through the crises of their lives they learned to take God at His word, to be patient, to be faithful, and to be thankful.

The altar and the tent were the characteristic features of life for the patriarchs. The altar symbolized their utter dependence on God; the tent symbolized their lives of pilgrimage. We too are strangers on this earth, bound for an eternal resting place beyond this earth. Let us face the crises of our lives with humility, trust, patience, and hope.

So, humble yourselves under God's strong hand, and in his own good time he will lift you up. You can throw the whole weight of your anxieties upon him, for you are his personal concern.
—1 Peter 5:6, 7, Phillips.